TRAVELS WITH TURTLE

TRAVELS WITH TURTLE

Oregon to Nova Scotia and Return

Harriet Denison

Library of Congress Number: 2003099732
ISBN: Softcover 1-4134-4381-8

This book was printed in the United States of America.

To order additional copies of this book, contact:
Xlibris Corporation
1-888-795-4274
www.Xlibris.com
Orders@Xlibris.com

23263

Orientation for readers who like details:

Temporal: The trip took place between September 6 and November 6, 2000.

Spatial: The map will help the reader follow the progress of the journey as described in the text. It does not trace every mile, but only indicates each stopping place of one night or more. Images on the map hint at highlights that occurred in each region.

Historical: The Family Ties chart will help with the family relationships. It is not intended as a full genealogical chart, but only includes relatives and ancestors mentioned in the text and some spouses and occasionally connecting parents.

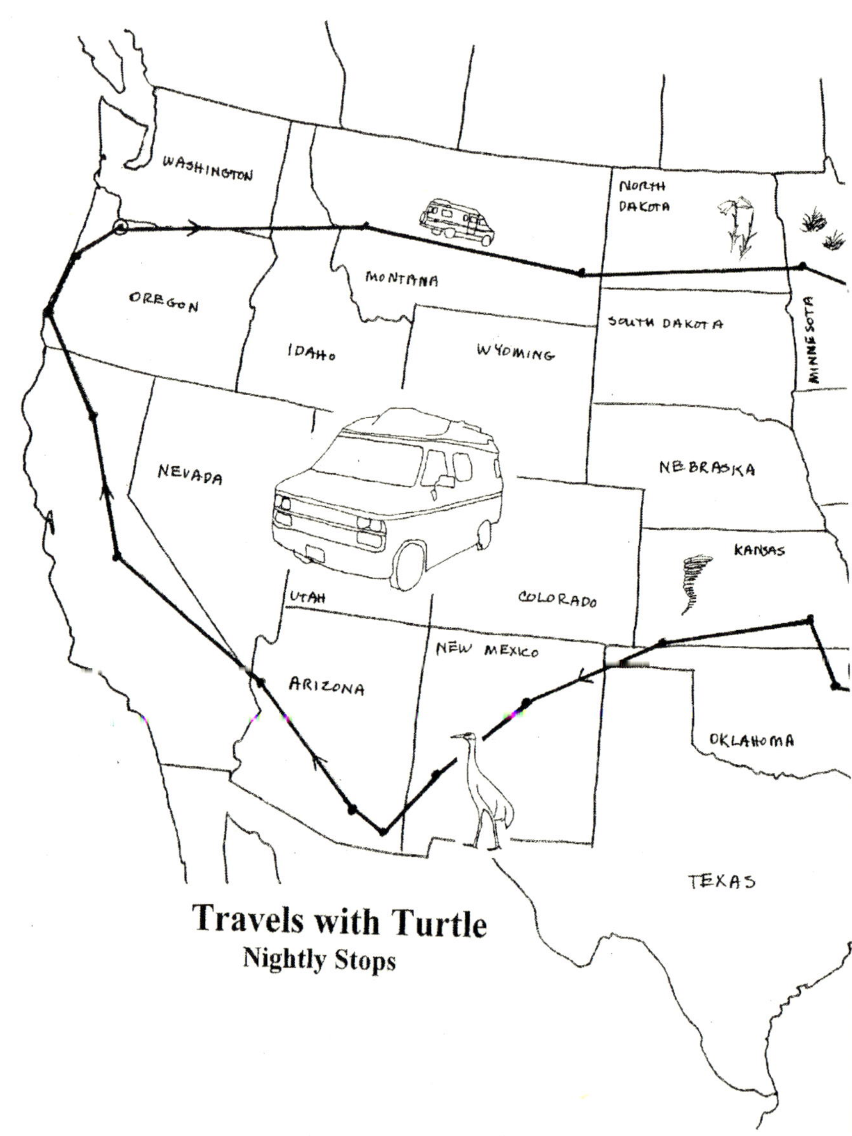

Travels with Turtle
Nightly Stops

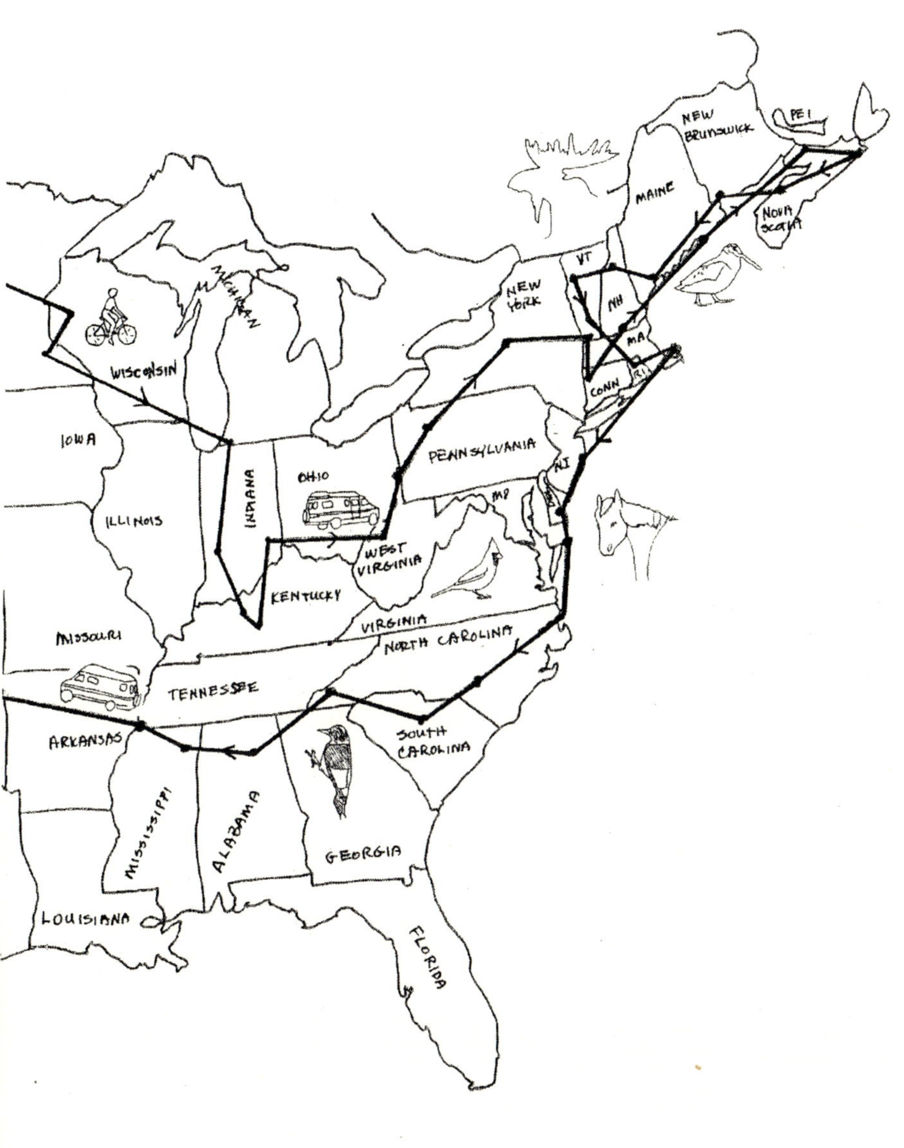

NEW BRUNSWICK
PEI
MAINE
NOVA SCOTIA
VT
NH
MA
RI
CONN
NEW YORK
MICHIGAN
WISCONSIN
IOWA
ILLINOIS
INDIANA
OHIO
PENNSYLVANIA
NJ
MD
WEST VIRGINIA
KENTUCKY
VIRGINIA
NORTH CAROLINA
MISSOURI
TENNESSEE
ARKANSAS
SOUTH CAROLINA
MISSISSIPPI
ALABAMA
GEORGIA
LOUISIANA
FLORIDA

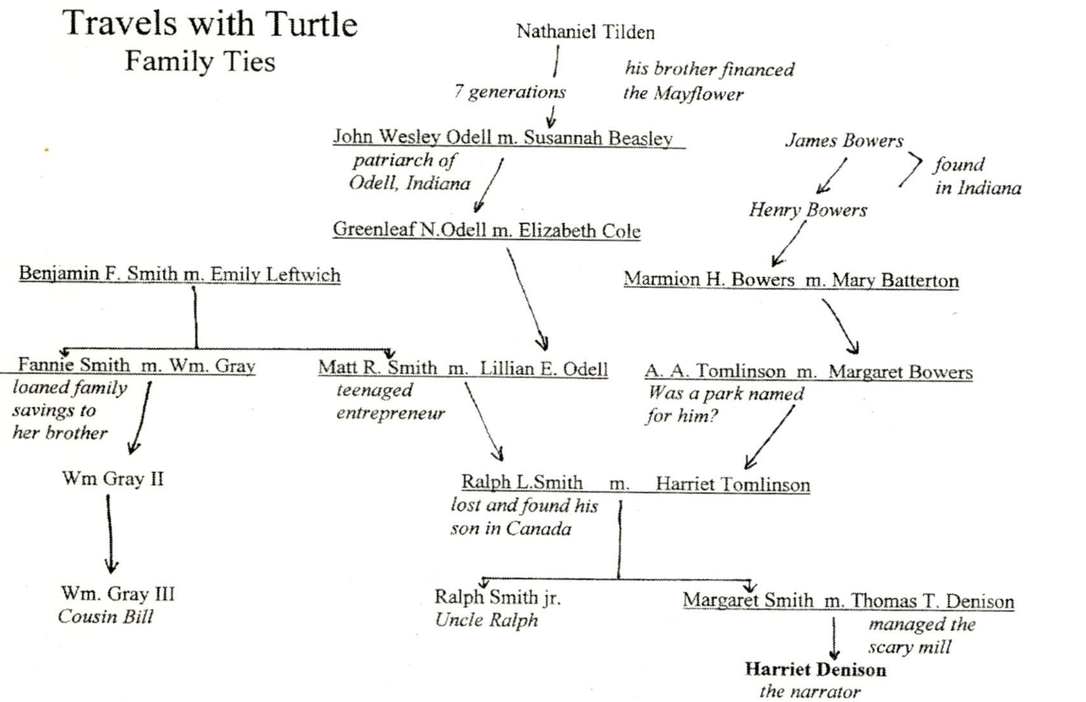

Travels with Turtle
Family Ties
Nathaniel Tilden
7 generations
his brother financed the Mayflower
John Wesley Odell m. Susannah Beasley
patriarch of Odell, Indiana
James Bowers
Henry Bowers
found in Indiana
Greenleaf N.Odell m. Elizabeth Cole
Benjamin F. Smith m. Emily Leftwich
Marmion H. Bowers m. Mary Batterton
Fannie Smith m. Wm. Gray
loaned family savings to her brother
Matt R. Smith m. Lillian E. Odell
teenaged entrepreneur
A. A. Tomlinson m. Margaret Bowers
Was a park named for him?
Wm Gray II
Ralph L.Smith m. Harriet Tomlinson
lost and found his son in Canada
Wm. Gray III
Cousin Bill
Ralph Smith jr.
Uncle Ralph
Margaret Smith m. Thomas T. Denison
managed the scary mill
Harriet Denison
the narrator

September 6, 2000, Oregon

Turtle rumbled east on I-84 through the Columbia River Gorge, her fat little body loaded for our two months on the road. The tight harmony of Cream filled the cab and I sang along with their great liberation song: "I'm so glad, I'm so glad. I'm glad. I'm glad. I'm glad."

At Hood River, Turtle and I left the Portland clouds behind the Cascade Mountains and welcomed the September sun of eastern Oregon. I love the rumble of the road, the whoosh of the wind, the sense that I am moving, moving. I wanted to drive, drive, drive. All I had to do was keep my hands on the wheel, watch the scenery, listen to my book tapes and let my mind wander.

The previous fall, I'd traveled to the Midwest for five weeks. It was my first real road trip in Turtle and we had a great time. No imposed deadlines, no obligations, only possibilities and an open road. In my youth, I loved to backpack, free to roam in unpopulated wilderness. As I approached sixty, I adapted my wanderlust to my age and enjoyed Turtle's spartan comforts.

On my return home, I knew I was hooked. On this trip, I had things to do, or at least things I *could* do. I still had fifteen states to visit. I signed up for a conference in Connecticut and an Elderhostel in Provincetown, which put my friends at ease when they asked why I was going. The real truth was: because. Because I could take two months for myself. Because I love seeing my country from the lesser-traveled routes. Because I know everybody isn't like me and I want to step into their worlds. Because at home, there is always something I can do that is important, useful and productive and I wanted some time to be invisible, unimportant and unscheduled. I could even skip those commitments I'd made if I felt like it.

Along the way, I could visit wildlife refuges. I was a novice birder and was marginally familiar with the birds of my area but I would be passing through places where birds rare in the northwest should be found in abundance. I expected many new encounters. And, of course, it's the serendipitous adventures that are the most fun. What was out there waiting to be discovered?

When I first saw her, I knew Turtle was right for me. She was white, with a saucy blue stripe along her side and she packed into her seventeen feet all I needed: a bed in the back, a tiny galley, generous storage and a biffy for those stops when the weather is too miserable to climb out to go to a public rest room. When the biffy bi-fold door is open, the bed area is closed off and is very private so I can camp anywhere and Turtle looks like an empty truck.

Turtle is a girl. She has soft, curving lines, making her wind friendly and gas efficient. On my first trip with her to the San Francisco Bay area, I waited for the universe to tell me her name. The friend I was visiting told my next host, who was worried I would pull up to her Castro district condo in a full sized bus, that I was like a turtle, my home on my back, small and compact. Coincidentally, I was reading *The Bean Trees* by Barbara Kingsolver, in which one of the main characters was a little girl named Turtle. Then I found a fat, purple and black stuffed turtle in a gallery with a tag describing all the turtles in mythology. I bought it and put it on her dashboard. The universe had spoken.

I like people but I'm quite happy by myself for days at a time. I keep a journal when I travel, which takes the edge off long periods of solitude. It's there when I need to whine, which I do a lot on a long trip. Short conversations and eavesdropping take on heightened significance, as do scenery changes and mind-wanderings. Remember that one. I'll write it down at the next stop. I've always had an active imagination, able to take insignificant incidents and blow them out of proportion, or entertain myself with linguistic contortions based on a sign that strikes me funny.

However, I did worry about being alone too much. When I traveled through Asia, I remember feeling as if I were inside a bell jar looking out at the world but unable to interact due to both language and cultural barriers. Sometimes, that's fine and feels safe. I like anonymity in a crowd, less stressful for me than talking with strangers, but there comes a time when I tire of my own company. The only problem is when I do find a willing person, I babble on like an overfilled balloon deflating, about those tiny things that seem to need saying until I say them, after which they seem way too trivial, but it's too late.

I never have been good at light conversation and after almost sixty years, I have accepted that I am what I am. I do wonder about people I meet, and many questions occur to me after we've completed whatever utilitarian things we have to say and I'm back in Turtle. I know people who never think twice about a conversation once it's over, but I go over everything. Keeps my brain occupied on a long drive, but leaves lots of questions.

I had rehearsed that first travel day in my mind all summer, worried that I couldn't keep up a rapid pace if I had to. I planned to use major roads until Minnesota to get past the familiar miles I'd covered the year before. At the end of my first driving day I had set a personal record, 577 miles in twelve hours, including many stops for food, a short walk or some yoga. I was well into the Rocky Mountains, past Missoula, Montana on I-90, and I had proved to myself that I could cover ground.

The next morning, patches of fog backlit by the rising sun blanketed the road. I played peek-a-boo with the rays as the road slinked though the hills and mountains. Mid-morning, I crossed the Continental Divide east of Butte and celebrated with a whoop. Covering ground. On my way.

I stayed on I-90 and coasted down the Rockies and into rolling hills and open brush land of the eastern Montana prairie. At Greycliff Prairie Dog City State Monument, west of Big Timber, I pulled off. The park was closed due to the high fire danger so I parked Turtle outside the chained gate. When I climbed out of the cab, the September heat enveloped me like a steamy blanket. I do love air conditioning on those hot prairies. Grassy land pocked with mounds of dirt surrounded the interpretive display at the top of a rise inside the park and I set off up the vacated road. Hundreds of prairie dogs watched me left and right. The furry observers sat on their haunches, forefeet limp. Some were on mounds and some on flat land but when I turned my head in the direction of the closest, I only caught a glimpse of a fuzzy tail as it dived out of sight. Squeaks of greeting preceded my passage, or I preferred to think they were greeting me rather than warning their friends that I was coming. I imagined I was the Queen on parade among loyal subjects and waved a royal hand to them all.

The mind enjoys itself. I have no control.

After reading the display and learning that these prairie dogs were the rare black-tailed prairie dogs protected by the Nature Conservancy, I retraced my steps and looked for the two types of entrances. They build their burrows with one opening in a mound and one on flat ground so any wind that blows across the higher hole pulls air into the lower entrance to ventilate the burrow. Clever little things.

Turtle waited for me beyond the gate, and I was glad to climb back into her cozy and very soon cool cab.

In Oregon, freeway rest stops are about an hour apart, 30 to 40 miles. One sign in Montana read "Rest Stop, 2 Miles. Next Rest Stop 212 miles." I'd hate to be driving in a car along that route with no trees or bushes to hide a modest lady's privates. A sign next to the cement path at another prairie rest stop said, "Rattlesnakes have been observed. Please stay on the sidewalks." I was a bit confused at that because I would have thought they preferred the hot cement to the well-watered and cool grass. Maybe later, the grass dries out and they hide in it. I have a lot to learn.

At Billings, I turned northeast on I-94 toward Glendive and then turned off at a sign for Makoshika State Park. I was near the eastern Montana border with the Dakotas, and close to the Badlands. The area deserved the name Makoshika, a Sioux name for "bad earth". Walls of tan sandstone were layered with loose red lava-like rock bits and weathered into outcrops and gullies. Bulges and washes hemmed the campground road. It is possible that one of those layers was laid down when Mt. Mazama in Oregon blew up and spewed volcanic ash into the atmosphere and formed Crater Lake in Central Oregon. In the coulees, gray-green sagebrush, cactus and yucca huddled where the last water flowed. Eroded capstones teetered above me, looking ready to plummet onto the road at any minute.

I shuffled Turtle around on my chosen night's site using the two levels stuck to the dashboard to tell me how close to level she was. She has to be fairly level when I use the propane option for the refrigerator, or risk burning out the cooling vent, which was not what I wanted this early in the trip. It also makes for a more comfortable bed. I set her up for the night: lit the frig; cranked open the roof vent; wrote down my mileage, route for the day and the park fee in my logbook. Even though I wanted no schedule, some rituals helped give order to the trip.

There was still lots of day left, so I unhitched my bike from the rack on the back and hopped on to follow the road further into the canyon for a close up view of the rock formations. Shadows walked across the stones, changing the appearance of the surfaces every few minutes. The road crawled up the steep wall at the head of the canyon. I ran out of energy 2/3 of the way up and stopped to recover from my exertion. Panting by the side of the road, I noticed a dirt path that curved along a ridge, so I pushed my bike a few hundred yards along it to a spot overlooking the watersheds to the west.

Settling on a comfy rock, I watched the sun edge toward the horizon. In one of my wilderness classes, I was told how to estimate the length of time until sunset. I held my hand at arm's length, fingers parallel to the horizon, and measured the number of finger widths between the sun's lower edge and the edge of the earth. Fifteen minutes per finger-width. I had two fingers left. Half an hour until the heat of the sun would abate.

The hogback ridges I could see looked like places to hike, high and open. Not that I wanted to take one then or even the next day but it was something to do when sitting on a mountain ridge. And if I did hike there, where would I go? What was behind that rocky outcrop or down in that valley, already cooling in the early shadows? I hike to find what's around the corner, but not that day. All I wanted was to sit and let the tension of driving all day drain away so I could appreciate the magnificent serenity surrounding me.

Too soon, the rosy disc touched the tops of the mountains, melted into the line between earth and sky, and then, slipped out of sight.

The evening air cooled my sweaty body as I coasted back to Turtle in the twilight. A thrill of companionship hit me as I rounded the last corner to see her plump body waiting for me.

The next morning I threw back my warm quilt and a cold blast of air shocked me awake. I dressed quickly, jumped in the driver's seat and chugged up the hill I'd biked the previous afternoon. Fifteen minutes of driving warmed Turtle up, and I parked her on a ridge facing east at Eyeful Vista, a propitious name for the event I was seeking. I settled into the right hand seat and propped my feet on the dashboard, a bowl of granola in my lap. Silhouettes of the hills emerged from the black void below.

The sky lightened. I munched my breakfast. Grey shapes transformed into yellow grasses, chartreuse shoots, gray rabbit brush and deep green juniper. I traded my empty cereal bowl for a cup of coffee and watched a diffuse salmon-colored horizon condense. A sharp sliver of brilliant orange snapped into view. The first rays hunched around the edges of the fluted hillsides to sharpen the striations in the water-worn sandstone. Ridges cut by eons of trickling water materialized, looking like lion's paws gripping the gully walls.

The sun was launched. I rinsed my cup and bowl, settled everything for driving again, and set out into another day.

I sped through North Dakota and camped at Buffalo River State Park, across the state line from Fargo, North Dakota. In my log I entered that I'd covered 419 miles and I was already in Minnesota. Moving along well, I'd say.

The shushing of the wind in the cottonwoods that shaded the campsites was gentle and friendly, very relaxing. I stretched my legs on the campground trail that wandered along the river lined with poplar, aspen and cottonwood. Bluebirds flitted through the brush, and near the river. A Piliated woodpecker flashed me from behind a dead tree trunk.

The trail broke into a wide field, my first experience on a trail cut in an expanse of native prairie grasses. In the northwest, hiking trails are built using shovels, axes, peevees, chain saws, maybe mules, gravel and picks. To build a trail there in Minnesota seemed to need only a wide lawn mower, and maybe extra blades if the ground-down granite rocks meant anything. Knee-high bunch bluegrass and chest-high clumps of a burgundy-colored Indian grass dominated the prairie vegetation. Fall wildflowers bloomed among blue-green shrubs: goldenrod, deep blue asters, yellow yarrow, and tiny flowers like our fiddleneck, only white instead of mustard colored. Splendid.

The park adjoins the Bluestem Prairie Scientific and Natural Area where 250 species of wildflowers and grasses are preserved and studied. Put this place on my list for a spring visit.

September 9, Minnesota

In the morning, the mosquitoes were thick and aggressive. Over my cup of coffee, I watched them fighting each other outside my windshield for their place in line. They must have known I would have to unplug my electrical cord before leaving. I plotted the fastest moves as I sipped: get out, unplug, coil and stow the cord and get back in bringing the fewest possible of the little devils with me. When I raced through my planned movements and slammed Turtle's door behind me, I had brought back the most eager of them. They lurked in the shadows. When I was driving and least able to fend them off, they bit my ankles. During my rest stops, I hunted them down, smashed them with a wet cloth and was irate when a smear of red appeared on the wall. I am embarrassed to admit, the passion of the hunt still runs in my pacifist veins.

Three and a half days into the trip, I was parked next to the St Croix River in Wisconsin. It was a great site, isolated, beautiful and hot. Turtle was the only vehicle in a parking lot for the little park. I only wished there had been some shade. I jammed my screens into the front windows for some air and put on my hiking shoes. The fishing trails offered me easy access to the river. A light breeze played on the surface and gave me some relief from the humidity as I strolled next to the soft burbling water. I could feel my driving shoulders relax. I loved the walk on the trail tramped bare by the boots of thousands of people who fished in the half-light of dawn and dusk. A couple of years before, I had tried to learn the secrets of fly fishing, but after discovering how much there was to learn, I decided I'd use a line with no hook for the privilege of standing thigh deep in cool water on a remote stream. Walking that trail was almost as good.

Across from the campground, away from the river, another trail lead back into the brush. It was wider than a hiking trail but not wide enough to be a road. Curious, I nosed down it for a while. Then, nature called. I started to squat for a pee at the side of the trail and discovered that I was not alone. The mosquitoes dived in for tastes of my tender flesh. Suddenly, the trail didn't look that interesting, and the bugs drove me back into Turtle. At dusk, a swarm of ATV's buzzed out of those bushes and roared down the road. Now I knew what the trail was for. Lucky they hadn't come earlier.

I was listening to "Prairie Home Companion" on the radio when six vehicles with Minnesota plates rushed into my parking lot. The largest vehicle was a motor home. The driver seemed determined to park it parallel to the river, across several parking spaces. His maneuvering brought him perilously close to Turtle, and I wondered if this might have been his first outing with a new toy. I was seriously thinking of moving as the back bumper of the huge vehicle inched closer and closer to Turtle's side. I leaned forward in the passenger seat and couldn't see the driver in his mirror. How could he see me? Then, one of the women shouted, "Randy! Stop! We don't want to run over the only other person here!" She smiled at me in apology. When Randy finally turned off the motor, the rest of the SUV's and tent-filled station wagons crowded in behind him and around me. Men and women in their forties pulled out folding chairs, hefted ice chests onto the picnic tables and assembled tents.

Then I heard, "Beer!" One of the men, maybe it was Randy, stepped out of the motor home with two six-packs held over his head, and marched them to a picnic table. People abandoned what they were doing and grabbed a can. They laughed and punched arms and looked as if they were having a great time, though I couldn't hear what they were saying. Garrison Keillor had started his monologue on the radio, but I wondered if the real thing might be more entertaining. These were real Minnesotans in their native habitat. Were they uptight Lutherans, each with a unique quirk like in Lake Woebegon? I turned off the radio and eavesdropped. They tipped up their cans, told good-natured jokes that I didn't understand though I could hear most of the words. They laughed and rocked back on their camp chairs. Maybe they were old jokes re-worked, or maybe my sense of humor was on a different plane. After all, I reasoned, I don't hang out with the beer-drinking group at home and anyway, I was probably not in the best position to catch the regional nuances. Disappointed, I flipped the radio back on to hear the end of Keillor's monologue.

Later, I ran into one of the women.

"What is this group?" I asked.

"Oh, it's a softball team. Senior league. These guys have been playing at the tournament nearby for over ten years. It starts tomorrow and ends Sunday."

"Everyone seemed to know what they were doing when you all arrived."

"Oh, yes. We stay at this park every year. When we started, they would party all night, but now they can't keep up the pace. Had to choose between the games or the party," she said

"And the games won?" I asked hopefully.

"Yeah. The guys won't admit it, but they've slowed down," she chuckled.

I envied the fun they were having even if I didn't understand why their verbal jousting was not as hilarious as they made it seem. Maybe I was a little lonesome out there far from friends. I'm not a party person, but I've spent time with old friends I knew so well we didn't need to tell the whole joke, only the punch line because everyone knew the story. Those were good times. This wasn't my party and I felt a little intrusive. Even though I had arrived first, I moved to the other side of the small parking area to give us both more privacy.

When the air cooled by eleven, the sedate party was over and we all slept.

Next to the Gandy Dancer Trail in Webster, Wisconsin, I slathered myself with bug juice, set up my bike and pedaled out of the parking area. The trail was built on an old railroad bed and was flat, straight and seemed to disappear only as the earth curved. No hills, and therefore no down and up, no curves, no obstacles. Not like the riding I usually do with lots of variation, shifting gears, heavy pedaling and some coasting to catch my breath. This seemed too easy but I needed the exercise, so I gave the flat trail a chance. It passed through stands of pine, alternating with open fields. Late summer blooms lined the edges: light blue asters, a thistle-like pink flower, another bullet-shaped blue flower not quite unfurled. It looked familiar, but this was not the habitat I knew and I was reluctant to name the flower. Later, I found the picture of a musk thistle in my wildflower book that looked right for the pinkish thistle. The picture of a gentian looked similar to the one I saw, but the range did not include Wisconsin. Some flowers must remain unnamed.

As long as I was pedaling, I generated a breeze that kept the mosquitoes at bay. When I stopped, it took about ten seconds for the first one to land, beak poised for the strike. They must have been letting each other know fresh flesh was moving down the path. Maybe they tapped out signals on the power lines with their tiny mosquito feet so the next ones were ready, salivating and alert. I can't imagine the disappointment when I rode on by. Those sad bugs then had to tap out the news, wishing the next ones in line better hunting.

After a good ride, I headed south on highway 35 and found an all-you-can-eat Sunday brunch cafe with a good crowd. Many were regulars if their girth was evidence. This was a find. Too often, I have looked for a Mom and Pop café in some small town, only to find it boarded up and all the local cars parked outside the fast food stop at the edge of town. I settled into my booth at the side of the dining area and tuned in for some eavesdropping. The fragrance of maple syrup wafted from the buffet, which looked well stocked and delicious: scrambled eggs, muffins, hash browns and stacks of pancakes, fruit salad. Juice pitchers were settled in shaved ice. A steady stream of diners wandered over for refills. But I resisted and ordered two eggs over easy and hash browns. I have the wrong mindset for buffets. I have to try small bits of everything. I may never be back to that table again. Then I have to eat it all so it doesn't go to waste. Thanks Mom. And then I go back for more of what was good and I end up eating way too much.

Most people were dressed casually, jeans and plaid shirts. Some looked more urban with brand name sweat shirts and shoes. One family with three generations had apparently been to church, dressed in nicer clothes. They brought to mind the old farmer's saying, "If you want to know what your wife will look like in 25 years, look at her mother." The middle-aged mother wore a loose dress that accommodated her spreading bulk while her lively teenaged daughter looked as she might have in her youth. The grandparents listened quietly to the conversation between the daughter and her parents, news of the game, and of friends.

"Yeah, Pete's the forward this year and if Friday's game is any indication, they're going for the cup this year."

"And Marylou is getting so big she can't hardly get in the car. She's due in ten days, thank the Lord."

At another table: "Mom took a hot dish over to her last night and she seemed OK. We keep an eye on her now Jack's gone. I don't think she eats well but she wouldn't think of asking for help."

Talk at the other tables was of families, high school friends, neighbors and weddings. The feeling was intimate, comfortable, joking and with a concern for people in the community. No one looked anxious to rush off to somewhere else.

And I was envious of this close community, of that caring I saw among the diners. Part of me wanted to be a part of that circle. But I was not brought up in a small town, though I have lived in rural places for short periods of time. I did not like that everyone knew everyone else's business. Not that they knew, but that it was of such interest because there wasn't much else to do but talk about who wasn't a part of the conversation.

Time to mosey into St Paul.

That evening, I chattered away with my friend Carol while my clothes dried in her basement. We had become friends while we both worked for a nonprofit organization, and had left about the same time. Our lives had changed but our friendship had not. I was lucky to catch her between trips and enjoyed my brief visit.

By the next morning, I was ready for the next leg of my trip. My goal was to get around Chicago and up into Michigan. I may not want to live in a small community but big cities are frightening to me. Heavy traffic, noise, confusing signs, angry drivers. I'll take a medium sized town, more anonymity and less traffic.

I was listening to a book based on Celtic myths and stories, which seemed to fit the wispy fog and eerie light of the early morning. The landscape was flat with few towns to break the miles. Several times I had to revise my course to avoid the severe thunderstorm that was causing chaos in Chicago. After hours of driving in thick traffic and pelting rain my brain was fogged. Michigan. Wisconsin. All those i's and n's confused me. At dusk, I pulled into a jam-packed toll plaza, and the tired woman who took my money confirmed with a chuckle that I was headed back toward Wisconsin, not Michigan. At the next overpass, I turned around waded back through the traffic to find the correct exit.

I finally took the first Michigan exit at 9:40 pm., way past when I like to stop driving. 577 miles was a hard day when so much was spent in heavy traffic and bad weather. Since I was heading back south the next day, I can safely say Michigan was the state I spent the least time in, but it still went onto to the list of states I had collected.

Why collect states? Years ago, Carol, my friend in St. Paul, happened to mention that she had been in almost all the states. When I counted, I was dismayed at the number I had never visited. What had I missed? What surprising places and eccentric people were waiting for me to discover, like the prairie trails and Eyeful Vista I'd just encountered. What misconceptions did I have, gleaned from books or media programs? I guess learning that Prairie Home Companion does not encapsulate the people of Minnesota was one important discovery. When I was teaching in Africa, the only news about my town that made the Oregon papers was about a murder trial, sensational because it involved a Peace Corps volunteer. My mother wrote in every letter how worried she was for my safety. Full of murderers, she concluded about my sleepy town, though I rarely heard a thing about the trial. On my trip through the United States, I hoped to discover for myself at least some tiny truths.

Then again, collecting states as pursuit appealed to me. Who can explain why anyone collects things or experiences? When I'm done with the states, I will be able to say, "I've been in all 50 states" to which my listener will gasp. We introverts enjoy our moments in the limelight.

September 12, Indiana

I was due in Massachusetts for a conference on the 21st, but I had made such good time, I had a few days for a detour. Kentucky looked appealing. The sun tried to break through at the Kankakee Wayside in Indiana, where I got some brochures for local events. I was dismayed to find I had missed the 22nd Annual Valparaiso, Indiana Popcorn Festival. Yes, Orville Redenbacher is from Valparaiso. The festival had been held on September 9, and featured the Popcorn Queen and Cutest Baby pre-festival events, story time with "Miss Patricia" and the Ag Day Kiddie Tractor Pull. Were they using kiddie tractors, or did they put those tots on full sized John Deeres? I would never know.

In Watford City, North Dakota the previous fall, I happened to park on a side street facing the main thoroughfare, which was not very busy. When the sheriff set up barricades right next to Turtle, I discovered I was in the front row for the kiddie parade celebrating the Fall Festival. At 11:00 am the costumed kids came streaming out from behind an old brick building to my right. Beribboned tricycles and chubby pinto horses carried kids of all ages. Other kids were tied to helium balloons, carrying limp cats, leading decorated dogs or pulling red wagons loaded with little brothers and sisters. The two leaders sped full tilt down the street chased by someone's mother.

"Slow down, Billy. Robert, slow down. Wait for the little kids. You're going too fast." The excited boys had made the parade into a race and did not respond to her entreaties. In a moment, the whole parade flashed by me and disappeared behind the building to my left. As I started to get out and explore the town, Billy and Robert re-appeared, speeding in the opposite direction, having turned around at the end of the street for a second pass. But in their lathered enthusiasm they still had not heard the woman chasing them. The kids were strung out, the laggers unable to keep up the frantic pace. The ribbons were drooping, and the kids had been busy popping the balloons until most were only lumps of limp rubber that bounced along at the end of their strings. Except for those eager leaders, it was the slow motion in reverse version of the first parade.

After the Watford City parade, I wandered into the recreation center for the auction I'd seen advertised on a flyer in the hardware store. Townspeople were selling themselves off to each other to raise money for something. The ones on stage hammed it up when the auctioneer named their attributes and the services they offered. Some were greeted with whistles. One woman seemed shy but was applauded loudly. Her reserve relaxed and she was able to wave as the bidding rose, and smiled when she was actually bought.

To one side of the gym, I saw some small tables with signs on them. I wandered over to discover that they were commercial sales tables set up to accompany the meeting of the local emu growers taking place an adjoining room. They were selling lotions and cosmetics. One had graphic pictures of a teenager with gruesome burns that were cured (before and after pictures) with emu oil alone. The sales lady promised it could cure any skin disease or erase any scar and I bought the smallest bottle for $15 out of curiosity. It smelled like old chicken fat when I tried it later on a patch on dry skin and had the same effect.

As I stood at the side of the gymnasium watching the activities, voice came from over my right shoulder.

"Hi, there," a robust man in casual garb said. "What do you think of all this?" He pointed to the tables of emu products.

"Interesting. I never knew emus were so unique."

He didn't rush to the point, but soon, he said, "Ever think of raising your own emus? You can do quite well with only a few birds."

"Is that so?" Where was he going with this? He kept to my

side. I'd turn to face him and he'd move around behind my shoulder again.

"Yep. I started with just a few eggs, and now I've got quite a herd. In fact, I've got some fertile eggs for sale, in case you'd like to try your hand. We're trying to build our supplier base so we can meet the demands that are growing."

"How much would an emu egg run?" Like I could see an emu chick tucked away in Turtle while I finish my trip.

"Good blood lines will run you $50 or so. If you're patient, it's better than buying a breeding pair that'll run you $1,000 and up. The market is still developing for the meat. It's really low in fat. It's going to be hot with everyone worried about cholesterol. You can get in on the ground floor."

I had my doubts. I'd never seen emu meat for sale. How would you even get one of those gargantuan thighs in a normal oven? And wouldn't it be all dark meat? People like white meat. And the man was closing in on my shoulder, making me a bit nervous. I thanked him and moved on. I wondered if all emu raisers were like him. It sounded like a Ponzi scheme to me. Raise emus to sell the next batch of hopefuls so they could do the same.

And now think what I had missed in Valparaiso.

Another rest stop brochure from the Tippecanoe County Historical Society announced the Feast of the Hunter's Moon, October 14-15. I could mine for family facts at the historical society. Not long after I began writing, I became curious about who I was, really. What of me did I invent, and what was passed on in the subtle ways families do? I wanted to know about my ancestors and had compiled data from various researchers and found I had quite a bit, but there is always more to learn. I carried my genealogical data with me, in case I happened to be in an area where I could do research. Several ancestors were born or died in the area and I thought the Tippecanoe County Historical Society in Lafayette, Indiana might hold some secrets.

It didn't, so outside the building, I studied my map and discovered Odell, Indiana was only twenty miles to the southeast. Odell is the family name of my maternal grandfather's mother, so I dug into my files to see what might be worth investigating in Odell. I found that in 1832 John Wesley Odell, my ancestor, settled on 800 acres of land in Brown County, Indiana and spawned a clan that named the town after him. He died there in 1876. A distant cousin had written:

> Determined to build for Susannah the home she deserved, he hauled timber thirty miles and built a large colonial type house. On this farm, they planted a grove of walnut and hard maple trees and near the house a bountiful orchard. As a signal of hospitality, they planted fruit trees in the alternate corners of the rail fence along the road. There, neighbors could help themselves to cherries, peaches, apples and pears in season.

From Dr. Francis Beasley Odell and Twila Birnie Shafer, Descendants of the Sutton-Beasley Family of Brown County, Ohio, 1946, p. 59.

Could some remnant of his farm still be here? I headed for Odell to see if anything recognizable remained after 125 years.

This was corn country. Fields full of ripe ears stretched in every direction. Acres and acres of standing, dry corn. The raspy rattle of the corn leaves made my hands feel dry and called to mind that lotion especially made for corn huskers. Cars on their way from Lafayette to Attica whizzed by the tiny highway sign that said "Odell" near the intersection of state highways 28 and 25. No population noted on the sign. No incorporation date, but it matched the spot on the map. I pulled off the highway at a tiny settlement with two main streets set at right angles, each not more than two or three blocks long, lined with old houses under mature maple trees. This must be the Odell, Indiana I was seeking.

I parked Turtle on an old cement slab beside what must have been a small general store. The windows and doors were boarded shut and the whitewash was thin and worn through. The heap of cement blocks in front had a metal pole stabbed in the middle with a "No Smoking" sign in red and white where the gas pump had been mounted. I looked around for someone who might know something about Odell, but the town was quiet. Not even a dog wandered down the street. The general store hadn't served a customer in so many years the painted sign had almost faded entirely away.

The trees grew along the streets, not in a grove, so I didn't think they could be the ones planted by my ancestor. How long will a maple or a walnut live? A lot can happen the years since John Wesley Odell's death in 1876.

A few of the residences looked occupied, tidy, with some flower pots in the yards, curtains on the windows, but most houses and a two-story warehouse with broken windows were slowly sinking under the heavy ivy vines that covered them.

What a disappointment. I wanted to find a prosperous town and a plaque commemorating my ancestor. There was nothing left of his house and property as far as I could tell. Did his descendants move on west, or did they stay with the land? Did they have to sell their land like so many other family farmers? Were his fruit trees pulled down to add to the cornfields that now encroach on that dying town? A number of fields I'd passed had small yellow and green signs posted next to the road with identification numbers on them. Were they growing genetically altered corn? I wondered. Did corporate corn surround me? Corporations need fewer farmers. Perhaps the little community had been deserted, to melt back into the soil, soon to be run over by another corporate cornfield.

Later, at home, I discovered I had records for where only four of the fourteen children of John Wesley Odell and Susannah died, and one did die in Indiana, but the town was not noted. Did his line stay on the homestead? Answer one question and another arises.

September 13, southern Indiana

I had brunch at the Black Buggy Restaurant, Bakery and Gift Shop in Washington, in the southwestern corner of the state. The gift shop had the tourist-revised version of the Amish community for sale with an Amish quilt or two here and there among a lot of commercially produced things: wooden toys, cutesy bears dressed for all occasions and peach baskets full of candies. Nothing new, but lots of it. Time to eat.

The dining room was full of tourists and locals, but no people dressed like Amish except the staff. At first I thought the thin woman at the table in front of me with straight pulled-back hair was trying to convert the other one. She leaned forward and talked a blue streak. I caught "the Lord", "Reverend (someone) says . . .," "A blessing," "The Devil." Her companion was quiet, listening. One of those eaves dropping devices spies use would have helped me catch more. Coming from a liberal neighborhood, I seldom hear that type of conversation. It was a new culture and I wanted to understand these women.

I got my soup and corn bread at the all-you-can-eat buffet. Obesity was the norm there—or do the fat people seek out those well-stocked places? Is that what drew me, or did I notice them only when I was feeling gluttonous?

When I returned to my table, the thin woman was still at it, speed-talking. The long, curly hair of the other woman hid her face from me but occasionally she would gesture, palms up, with her dry, red hands, waiting for the Word from above. I heard her say He told her to do something. Does she talk with Him often?

I got my salad. The tables were almost all full in four crowded rooms. Creamy faced teenaged Amish girls with their starched bun hats served beverages and cleared the tables for the next sitting.

Finally, Curly was talking. She was saved and so were her children, a blessing it was. And you should have heard what her son said just last week when he was baptized. Out of the mouths of babes. What a miracle. She also leaned forward. Their intensity was hard, brittle. I had to turn for relief to the table of four thickening women in their thirties, with heavy eye shadow, laughing and playing at eating each others' desserts. On my right, a Marine with a shaved head and his quiet mother and sister were cleaning their plates. Was this a farewell meal or were they just quiet diners?

Time to find the hot food, scrambled eggs, sausage, fried chicken and very good garlic mashed potatoes. In the other hand, desserts, a taste of everything on a big plate.

The women at the table in front of me never paused. When one was talking, the other reinforced her piety with Amens and the occasional touch on the arm of her companion. They bemoaned agnostics. No point in even talking to them. They won't listen.

But I was listening. Until the last comment, I was gathering information, a recorder, open to a new experience. But with the last comment, it became personal. The thin woman facing me probably would disdain me. I could imagine her as part of a witch-burning crowd, or one who shouted outside of a local women's reproductive health clinic, knowing in her heart she was right to save those sinners.

Maybe this was really a very nice woman if I gave her a chance. Maybe if we were neighbors and we traded canned peaches and watered each other's lawn during vacations we would discover each other's common humanity, but I could not conjure up a positive image of the tightlipped women so sure of her beliefs.

It was time to leave for a more sublime environment.

Driving helped. I was listening to a good mystery, and the road was not busy, although I did get tired of the cornfields, rolling like an ocean of corn. By afternoon, the tight-lipped woman was just another experience. Did I really expect them all to be to my liking? I wondered if women like those did live near me. Was I in such a rut at home that I didn't run into them? Are my antennae tuned to a different channel when I'm in my own element? Even in conservative rural Oregon, I never had heard such a conversation. Was I listening?

Later in the trip, I found in a rest stop in New York a picture of The Last Supper laminated onto a section of a log. Passing over any judgment about tackiness, or about the appropriateness of selling such religious things in a shop on state property, I just had to laugh.

The campground at Nolan Lake, Kentucky was built by the Corps of Engineers and properly located on a lake, not in the middle of cornfields, like my previous night's campground which felt very strange. They were about to close for the season and only a few campers were set up on the sites. My kind of place. All the amenities but few people. I've never liked being parked for two weeks in the same spot, cheek by jowl with strangers. At this time of year, campgrounds were appealing.

After dark, I walked the campground roads that swooped gracefully around the lakeshore. The silky evening air was a perfect temperature, not hot, not cool. Soft night noises: cicadas, frogs, the rustling of lightly blown leaves. Campers murmured, hypnotized by the sparks of their dying fires. I stood at the edge of the lake and watched a fat harvest moon float up over the sheltering hills and through streaked clouds to cast a shimmering apricot path on the water. A gentle night.

In the morning, I took a bike ride further around the lake than I had walked and found an interesting trail. I dropped my bike and hiked into the forest of small oaks to see where it would lead. In a grove of small birches, I looked up, listened for new bird songs, and watched for flashes of feathers. Ahead, I could see that the trail crossed a small gully on a wooden footbridge. A tree had fallen onto the bridge, breaking it in two, and I approached the steeply slanting section. I thought, "Be careful. This is a dangerous angle. It could be slippery."

In the middle of that thought, my feet flew forward. Something huge smacked my bum and flash of pain roared up my back. I felt totally disoriented and found myself sitting down, my legs in front of me. I couldn't breathe. I propped myself rigid, palms on the slimy wood. *Inhale*, I commanded. Nothing happened. Panic overwhelmed me as I began to suffocate. *Inhale.* Finally, I gasped as my ribs obeyed and the welcome air raced into my pleading lungs. Now the pain was everywhere. I was afraid to move; afraid I'd broken something. Never in my life had I been seriously hurt. I'd taken first aid classes but I was trained to be the rescuer, not the victim. I knew to suspect a broken coccyx after a fall like I'd taken. Was mine broken? The pain settled in my mid-back. *What can I do?*

As the pain subsided, my brain churned with questions. What if I couldn't sit to drive? What if I had broken something? What if I couldn't get help? What if I died there, leaving only my poor bones to be found in the spring? I could handle that, if only I would expire quickly. But maybe I wouldn't. Bummer.

Get a grip. This could be serious.

When the pain subsided enough to consider moving, I rolled onto my hands and knees with the care and attention of a yoga move. No added agony, so I slowly rose. I found my bike and rode carefully back to Turtle, still alert for new pain.

I managed a careful shower, and decided it might not be the end of the trip, but with time to think, I knew I could create vivid scenarios of middle-of-the-night emergencies from slowly developing inflammations, bone cracks or muscle rips, real or not. To shut up the nagging worry, I turned Turtle toward Bowling Green, the nearest town of hospital size.

I anxiously watched a middle-aged doctor with salt-and-pepper hair examine the X-rays.

"No broken bones," she said, "but you'll have a lovely bruise. I'll prescribe some pain killers and anti-inflammatories in case you need them."

Hooray for my mature woman's well padded butt. One saved coccyx.

She advised ice then heat. I filled the prescriptions and added them to my traveling pharmacy, hoping I could hold off taking anything until I reached the campground near Mammoth Caves. Once settled there, I bought a bag of ice for the first treatment.

I never bothered to find out what muscles are in play when you turn over in bed. Now I know. Quite a few, and it isn't easy when none of them want to be used for the task. During one of my waking periods after a turn, I thought, I'm almost sixty. What kind of an old person will I be? Not a happy one if I have to put up with pain like I had that night. I vowed to keep exercising, doing yoga, lifting weights and eating well, though some of that would have to wait until I healed. I crossed my fingers and slept until I had to turn again.

Before my tour of the caves the next morning, I walked on an easy trail through a young forest of beeches, poplars and maples gripping their still-green leaves. Mindful of my bruised back, I felt fairly mobile.

Back at the reception center, people were gathering for the next cave tour. When I was young, we often visited the Oregon Caves, which was near my grandmother's ranch in southern Oregon. We always took visitors there since it was the only tourist attraction we knew. My younger brother knew all the guide's jokes and I think the guides disliked having him along. He blew their favorite lines before they got to "Fat Man's Misery", a narrow passage, or "Tall Man's Lament", a hanging stalactite in the middle of a passage. The variety of formations seemed endless and I hoped to see more at Mammoth Caves.

Could I make it through an hour and a half more of walking? I watched a large bus pull up to the curb. The elderly tourists grappled their way down the high steps, several with canes. Even with my tender back, I thought I could keep up with them, so I bought my ticket. In Oregon, cavers could rent red coveralls for the tour, for protection and warmth. The Mammoth Cave complex stays at 54°F, so at that time of year, the temperature was about the same inside and out and I already had the right clothing.

Limestone underlies the Mammoth Caves region. Rainwater falls on the ground and seeps through the soil, picking up small amounts of carbon dioxide gas forming a weak acidic solution. The acid erodes the limestone forming a solution of calcium carbonate. The slow erosion over eons opened the underground caves we toured. The caves were explored first 4,000 years ago and the guides pointed out smoke smudges from earlier cave explorers who used pitch torches.

The tours available cover only a fraction of the 350 miles of surveyed passageways, and a possible 600 more miles remain unexplored. One tour does go into an area where there are stalactites and stalagmites. If the limestone solution slows down, as it would if it seeps through tiny cracks, and the water evaporates when sliding down an open surface, the solution of the dissolved limestone becomes stronger until it is saturated and must return some of the calcium carbonate to its solid form. In the Oregon Caves, we saw many stalactites hanging from the ceiling with a drop of water on the end. Directly below, a stalagmite showed where the drops fell. The possible formations depend on the surface over which the water oozes and can vary from creamy smooth walls to dramatic curtains, huge caverns to delicate spikes.

Near the cave entrance were the remains of the saltpeter processing works run by slaves during the War of 1812. Saltpeter, an ingredient in gunpowder, was boiled and filtered until the pure crystals could be packaged and shipped to gunpowder factories. Prices soared at the start of the war, but demand decreased after it was over. In 1837, the caves were developed for tourists and now, thousands of people tour them under the watchful eyes of the guides. I was tempted to touch the petroglyphs left by ancient tribes for the experience of touching something someone created thousands of years before, but the guides had warned us that the acid from fingers would have damaged them so I restrained myself.

As we moved through the dark passages, the guides turned on lights for the one we were entering and turned them off as we left. Even in the pitch dark, 130 forms of life manage to survive, some are visitors and some never leave the cave. We saw gray and reddish coloration on the limestone, which was one form of life. In the pools larger creatures like eyeless fish and the totally white cave crayfish have adapted to their environment. But the light and heat from leaving the lights on would have disrupted the fragile ecosystem.

In that environment, my sense of time and space went nuts. In one large cave, the guides had us plant ourselves carefully, and turned out all lights. We waited for our eyes to adjust. My mind began to hallucinate. I had no reference to orient myself. I could have been falling and I had to check the feeing in the soles of my feet to assure myself I was really just standing in a cave.

I taught chemistry at one time and can appreciate the time involved to form the caves, time beyond comprehension; time for solid rock to dissolve, for creatures to evolve and adapt to the strange environment. And now, with the increased air pollution, the rain is much more acidic, a serious threat to the cave ecosystem.

Halfway through the tour, we took a break. As I sat on the gritty floor, I stared up at the high water mark from a recent flood. First, I imagined I was sitting under the rush of water looking up twenty feet to the surface. Then, I imagined myself lost down there, like Tom Sawyer and his friends, with the water rising. Maybe I could find a dome where air is captured that I could breathe, like under an upturned boat. Or could I hold my breath long enough for the rush of the water to flush me into sunlight?

Why do I do that to myself?

September 15, Indiana again

On my map, the little red tent, the campground symbol, is printed to the west of Versailles, Indiana but the campground was two miles east. I discovered this after a scenic but unwanted detour. I think the mapmakers do that as a joke.

Suddenly it felt like fall. I had to wear my fleece and sweats to the shower, which took its sweet time to get warm. Standing naked, in a chilly fog from the running cold water, gritting my teeth until the hot water comes is one of those inconveniences that goes with the trip. The only thing Turtle does not have is a shower and shower experiences often show up in my journal, because I usually did some final writing before bed. The variations are infinite.

I will share only my most profound discovery regarding shower protocol: Wear shorts to the shower house when possible and no underwear. When you are finally clean and dry after a shower, you are still standing on a wet floor, if not in a puddle. Often, walls are dripping since only the most posh showers actually have curtains. When standing on one foot and pointing the moist toe of the other into the leg hole, the target area is wider in shorts. Practice standing on one foot before you go. You need good balance to get each foot through the leg hole without falling into a wet wall, drying the foot on the pants or dragging one pant leg in a puddle during the maneuver. Before perfecting my technique I arrived several times back at Turtle with a wet crotch or pant leg.

In spite of the new chill in the air that evening, Turtle was still warm from the driving, and still toasty as I unloaded my shower bag. I use thin towels so I can drape them on the back of the seat and they are dry by morning. My favorite towel has a print of Big Bird on it. The image always faces the seat so passersby would be unable to see my towel. Why am I self-conscious about the large silly avian? Sometimes I feel like my niece at about four. "Don't look at me!" she'd tell us. I am aware of being observed and I want to control what others know about me. Maybe it's because I peep into other people's lives. I want to observe them in their natural state, but not have them observe me in mine. It's the scientist in me. Any observer will disrupt the natural activities of observed animals, making it difficult to do studies. I have to catch myself sometimes and remind myself that I am not studying these creatures in nature. These are people, and I am a person. We can interact. We can talk. One friend told me once when I got on this tangent about watching and being watched, "I've got lots better things to do than worry about what you are up to." It didn't cure me.

While I ate my dinner snack, I listened to an old Radio Mystery Theater episode. Tinny voices. Dramatic music. Scary drama. The works. Like when I was a kid. She bludgeoned her abusive husband with a frozen leg of lamb, and then cooked it for dinner. No weapon could be found and she was never even a suspect.

My dinner was delicious: my last two tomatoes picked from Charles and Ursula's garden before I left home, a raw carrot, rice cakes, a raisin bread bun and juice. I rarely cook on the road. The smells linger and bears are attracted to them, though I did not worry there in the middle of Indiana about bears. But there are no pots to clean, either, using up water and filling up the waste tank. The substantial mid-day meal at Mom's Restaurant had filled me up and I was, as usual, camped far from any town.

On my morning walk, a flat and gentle one to favor my bruised back, the trail crossed and re-crossed a stream bed made up of palm-sized chunks of limestone full of fossil imprints: snails and clams and one Dalkon shield-shaped trilobite. This sediment was formed 380 millions years ago on the bottom of a tropical ocean which shifted north on the earth's restless tectonic plates. The other strollers didn't seem to notice them. Too common, I guess. I tucked two little souvenir pieces under my passenger seat with the pinecone from the St. Croix River.

East of Versailles, I passed tobacco barns full of bunches of huge yellow leaves drying in the rafters. Many small patches of tobacco next to the more modest houses were the source of some extra money for the family. Other homes in good repair along Hwy. 350 had large yards that were well kept and tidy. The lawns were huge, the size of fields themselves. In the center of each expanse stood a small, plain, rectangular house. One out of four lawns had someone driving around on a ride-on mower. The speed of the mower seemed in inverse proportion to the age of the driver. The teenager speeds so fast it's a miracle the cutter blades can catch the grass. And the older guy, what is it? A longing for his early years? He has his John Deere cap on and stares so intently at the line of cut, you'd think this year's profits hung on his lawn-mowing prowess. The lawns had few trees and no flowers. Just a lawn. Makes for a cleaner mow, I guess.

When I compiled my genealogical data, I discovered how many of my ancestors were merchants and professionals, lawyers, doctors or bankers. I traced the lines of my eight great-grandparents as far as I could go and I was able to trace all eight lines back to 1800 and everyone lived in the United States. I like the symmetry. Two ancestors sailed from England before 1650 and those were the most carefully document by professional genealogists. I love the hunt, but as with birds, accuracy is secondary.

I had the least information on the Bowers line, my mother's grandfather. Marmion Henry Bowers was born in Moore's Hill, Indiana, which lay about 15 miles north east of my Versailles campsite. He was a lawyer in Austin, Texas, where he lived with his wife Mary and five children: Henry, Mary, Margaret, Rizpah and Hayes. My mother had Mary Bower's ancestry traced to a revolutionary soldier so she could be a member of the Colonial Dames to please her father but the men's lines are not important to the Dames, so Marmion was the last person I knew of his line. I thought maybe there were some answers about his family in Moore's Hill.

Highway 350 skirts the edge of Moore's Hill, sucking the life out of the fading town. New houses with big yards lined the highway but two blocks away, big hardwood trees shaded Victorian houses in varying states of repair. Dogs roamed free, and a kid on a tricycle scooted over to the gravel shoulder to let me pass. A few stores in need of paint lined what had once been a thriving main street. Half of the stores were still in business, including a hardware store and small lumberyard. Sunbeams lit by floating dust shone in the windows of the vacated storefronts. A Bible college dominated the other side of the creek, but what I saw of the town didn't seem large enough to support a school of any size. Maybe there was more town somewhere that I missed but I since didn't see any municipal buildings that might contain records, I returned to the highway.

I had better luck at the library in Lawrenceburg, the Dearborn county seat. The public libraries in Indiana and the adjoining states have large sections for genealogical sleuths because the migration routes of early settlers passed through the area. In the file cabinet dedicated to local people, one folder was labeled BOWERS. Aha. An old newspaper article illuminated the life of Henry James Bowers, MD, of Marblehead MA, born about 1800, son of Reverend James Bowers. Married Rizpah Morgan (b. PA 1804), and all lived in the Lawrenceburg area in their later years. Their son, Marmion, graduated in Law from Indiana University and left for Texas in 1855. Bingo! Two more generations to pencil into my pedigree chart. And the mother's unusual name explains why Marmion named one of his daughters Rizpah.

Marmion's fourth daughter was named Hayes L. Bowers and Hayes is one of the family lines on my father's side, another braided path of relationships. I discovered I share common ancestors with both candidates in the Hayes-Tilden presidential election in 1876. This means, of course, that I am related to myself.

As the country was settled, land was the basis of wealth for many and the first settlers had the opportunity to claim acreage. My family records were traced through documents pertaining to land as well as births, marriages and deaths. Many of the women were also well educated so it was no coincidence that I grew up expecting to go to college.

September 17, Ohio

From Lawrenceburg I skirted Cincinnati and crossed southern Ohio near the Ohio River. Aside from the nuclear power plants strung along the river, it was a lovely pastoral drive. I spent the night deep in a canyon in West Virginia, at a well-developed public campground near Wheeling. Turtle and I backtracked into Ohio the next morning to do some more research on family places. We sped down the I-70 freeway in eastern Ohio working up to my second breakfast, listening to *Elvis is Dead and I Don't Feel So Good Myself,* Lewis Grizzard's book about growing up in the fifties and sixties. Maybe that set me up for what followed. I pulled off the freeway west of Wheeling, West Virginia. I looked around for a diner and felt as if I'd entered a time warp. The service station, they used to be called that and actually provided service, had a repair bay open, a car poised on the hoist, and no minimart. I pulled into the parking lot of the Omelet House Restaurant, a squat building with a tilted flat roof and long skinny bricks under the plate-glass windows that leaned into the sidewalk.

I slipped across the bouncy plastic seat of my booth with a view of the parking lot to the tune of "Kisses Sweeter Than Wine" emanating from the jukebox. I expected the waitress to be chewing gum, wearing a little ruffled apron, white shoes and have fat hair and an attitude. No attitude or gum but her starched uniform fit the era.

She took my order and left. A moment later, she returned loaded with plates balanced up her arm to the table of the only other diner, who sat across from me. The young man's eyes sparkled when she filled his table with his order of juice, grits, a waffle, bacon, eggs and toast. He pulled the grits forward. He pinched the butter out of the fluted paper cup and asked for another. He stirred the melting scoop of butter while he bounced up and down—stir, stir, bounce, bounce, add milk and sugar-stir-bounce-stir-bounce. Taste it. More milk. Stir, bounce. He was focused on his work with a smile on his face. I love watching an enthusiastic diner.

More ancestral investigations took me to eastern Ohio, but it was Sunday, and library research was not fruitful. I hoped I might find remnants of a family farm near Cadiz in Harrison County. My mother's paternal grandfather, Col. Abia Allen Tomlinson (1832-1913) was born in Harrison County. He served in the Fifth West Virginia Volunteers during the Civil War, ending the war as a Colonel. I knew his father was Thomas (1800-1860) and grandfather was Nathaniel (1772-1849), but my knowledge of the line ends there. According to a niece of Colonel Tomlinson's, the family came from Cadiz Junction, Harrison County. In a letter to another family researcher, she wrote this about the Colonel's father, Thomas Tomlinson:

> Grandpa must have been highly educated as his beautiful penmanship on his Will and on other papers show up. This house at Cadiz Junction was two years in building, making the brick in a brick kiln right on his farm and he was a prominent, wealthy farmer having plenty of help when necessity required to make the business a complete success. A beautiful home—Cadiz people used to say the next place to Heaven.

My AAA map did not show a Cadiz Junction, but Cadiz, Ohio looked like a substantial town and had to be near the junction. Certainly there were records that might help me find this place next to Heaven.

After being shunted off the freeway by a construction detour, I had a pleasant drive over hilly pastureland with friendly cows and quaint barns. Signs on the back road pointed toward Cadiz right up until the last one, which declared the road ahead was closed. Take this other detour. I was returned to the freeway, two exits east of where I had left it.

It was getting late in the day, so I changed direction to find Tomlinson Run State Park located at the tip of the West Virginia finger. One family legend credits Col. Tomlinson with persuading West Virginia to separate from Virginia at the beginning of the Civil War. Maybe in gratitude, they named the park after him. I sought proof.

Highway 7 to the north paralleled another section of the Ohio River. As I approached Weirton, West Virginia, the pastoral river scenery was spoiled by several power plants plunked on the river's edge. I entered Weirton from the south into dingy, narrow streets lined with three and four story brick buildings. Several bars were open, and a few men in grimy work clothes and somber faces stumped along on the sidewalks. Then the road entered an industrial area and climbed onto a viaduct that passed right through the middle of a gigantic roaring steel mill. On either side, enormous buildings of rusty metal threatened to devour me. Curling vents and pipes big enough for a car to drive through punched into their walls and added to the nightmare scene.

Once past the mill, I drove next to the trickle of the Ohio River and I wondered why I had just felt so afraid. A scene popped into my head. When I was about eight, my father proudly gave me a tour of the sawmill he was managing for my Grandfather Smith in Elgin, Oregon. We watched a heavy carriage thrust huge logs past a shrieking band saw. With every pass, a new plank fell onto a table with chains that pulled the planks past men who flipped them over and sorted them into piles. My tall father stooped down to my level, yelling in my ear over the rattling chains, shouting men and creaking carriages. He was trying to tell me what was happening. His closeness was reassuring, but I couldn't hear what he was saying, and the noise and rapid movements terrified me. I wouldn't let myself show him my fear. I felt the same tightly controlled fear driving through the steel mill in Weirton.

Looking back, I'm not surprised that I was able to control the impulse to panic. In many situations, this control of mind over emotions, has served me well. I've gotten lost while hiking and worked my way back to safety by assessing my situation with a conscious calm, controlling the urge to make a hasty and bad decision. One time, I was hiking by myself on a square-shaped trail early in the season, the last leg being at the highest altitude. Tired and late in the day, I encountered snow on the upper part of the trail. I could not trust finding the trail under the snow or seeing the trail blazes on the trees, which were far apart and not clear in the dim afternoon. I was tempted to forge ahead. According to my map I was only a mile away from my car. Another possibility was to strike out downhill following my compass, to where I knew the trail I had earlier walked had to be, saving considerable time if it worked out. I knew there could be a canyon or impenetrable brush in the way, requiring me to detour and increasing the chances of really getting lost. The best decision would be to retrace the trail I had just traversed in the last three hours, and not risk getting caught out overnight. With reluctance, I turned around to follow the known trail. I got back to my car exhausted and cold but safe.

It is this confidence that I will do the right thing when it counts most that gives me the freedom to travel alone as much as I do. I know and respect the risks in the adventures I undertake, and I do all I can to collect the knowledge and resources I might need along the way. Then I go, open to what comes along. Afterwards, I ponder any missteps to bring more information to the next venture.

With all my wandering, I covered 339 miles that day by the time I landed at Tomlinson Run State Park. It was perched on a hill surrounded by a hardwood forest of oak, cherry, beech, elms and ash. The park was well laid out, nicely trimmed and quiet when I arrived. A group of elderly park volunteers were hanging around the little store and registration building. Proud of their park, they each contributed quite a few days every year working where they were needed.

I asked if they knew who the park was named after.

"Well," said one of the silver-haired men in green pants and a hiking jacket, "There were lots of Tomlinsons around here. Still are. They didn't move far. But I don't know which one was The Tomlinson."

Another man chimed in, "I don't think the park was named after a person. It was named after the run, which has been here forever."

I suppose the local Tomlinson's were named after the run? I didn't voice my quirky thoughts. Some people don't understand when I'm not serious.

I filled out the campground form and gave my money to the uniformed woman behind the counter in the old store that served as the park office.

"Just a minute," she said. "There might be something here that would help."

She pulled out a thick sheaf of papers from under the counter. "Someone wrote this up a while ago. I haven't read it, but it's about the park. Maybe there's something in here about the name."

I thanked her and promised to return it. Then I turned to the watching group of elders. Though I knew they would think I was rather simple, I had to ask, "What is a run?"

A dignified gentleman took a moment to recover his surprise and then said, "It's all the area that a creek or a river drains."

I understood immediately. Very sensible, though my Webster's does not contain that exact definition. Where I live, we would call it a watershed. Tomlinson's Watershed doesn't have the same charm to it as Tomlinson's Run.

From the bundle of local history, I learned that the park was named for Tomlinson Run, as if the Run named itself. No one loses sleep around there over what particular Tomlinson named the run.

When I re-examined my records, I discovered that A. A. Tomlinson, as his family and friends knew the Colonel, enlisted as a Private when the war started. Where did that idea about his role in the separation of the states begin? Did I make it up after seeing the park on the map? I wonder if all genealogists read into sketchy information what they would like to see. Don't we all want to claim famous people as ancestors? There are, after all, many lowly enlisted men in all wars. And not every pioneer settled a plot of land that was situated in the middle of a metropolis years later, bringing good fortune to the descendents.

Colonel Tomlinson did do well after the war by settling in Kansas City, a thriving western town. He practiced law, bought some land that was eventually engulfed by the city, and helped start a number of Kansas City institutions like the U.S. Trust Company, of which he was the first president. But apparently, he did not have a park in West Virginia named after him.

I like walking without a light at night. It's a test of confidence when I am unable to see the ground, trusting it will be there when I take a step. Crickets, cicadas and frogs serenaded me on my evening walk. Guided by starlight on that moonless night, shadows of posts and trees seemed to move in my peripheral vision. I walked toward the other camping loop and as I approached a barrier and a "closed" sign, I remembered the car I had seen drive out from behind that sign earlier in the day. At the time, I wondered what it was doing back there if the area was closed. Did someone live there? Did the camp ranger know about the squatter? Cautiously, I proceeded and my imagination kicked in. What if someone else, like me was walking without a light? Would I know it? Would I see them or hear their footsteps? And what if they actually spoke to me? Ooooo.

I approached the brightly lit shower building. Odd, for a supposedly closed portion of the campground. Why does it need a light? Aha. I felt so clever finding them out, hiding someone down there. But then I walked into the illumination and felt exposed and vulnerable and hurried on to get back into the shadows. My fears about Appalachian poor folks surfaced: stereotypes of hillbillies, feuding and fighting, guns, illegal stills, black mustaches, floppy overalls and big rumpled hats. "Deliverance". I played the edges of self-inflicted terror until I saw the awning lights of a permanent trailer beyond the silhouettes of the trees where a trailer shouldn't be. Suddenly, I'd fallen off the edge of induced fear and it wasn't fun any more. Time to turn around and hurry back to my safe nest inside Turtle.

I like small spaces. After a long day or a scary walk, I can retreat to her tiny spaces and feel embraced and safe. The sleeping area is all mattress, and I keep the window curtains down. Behind the biffy door I have total privacy. I can use the biffy, brush my teeth or wash my face at the tiny kitchen area and no one can see me.

On that night, however, my nest was rather noisy. A roaring from the east took the edge off my feeling of safety until I checked my map and discovered that Pittsburgh was only 30 miles to the east. When the roaring stopped, I wondered if some mill had been doing something related to steel manufacturing. I was glad I wasn't any closer.

September 19, New York

Next stop, Niagara Falls. I braced myself for a disappointment. Films of the falls were magnificent, but adoration from the public has ruined many natural wonders. One of the oldest attractions in the U.S., Niagara Falls has a long history of attracting daredevil stunts: tight ropewalkers and people in barrels. Do honeymooners really flock there to just look at the falls? Sometimes I am surprised.

The main park and viewing area was pleasant. From behind the stone wall that kept eager tourists from falling into the pounding river, I imagined I was the first person to see it. Now that's worth contemplating. Imagine, trudging for months through wild land, seeing few if any people, and coming across this massive complex of waterfalls. Thrilling to see, but what if I needed to cross? A big detour.

But the nearby town was seedy. Solid tourist trap. Glitzy souvenir stores and a food mall that left me worried about food poisoning after downing a plate of lukewarm Chinese. I like souvenirs. I understand that impulse, but why buy something plastic made in China to remind you of a place that inspires poets, thrill-seekers and romantics?

I was pacing myself to arrive at the conference in Massachusetts in a few days, and did not want to waste my time in Niagara Falls when Seneca Falls, New York was nearby and the Women's Rights National History Park promised to be a more satisfying stop.

The volunteer at the Seneca Falls information booth said the exhibition building was closed when I arrived, so I made my way to the campground, which I found after another unplanned scenic tour. I was exhausted and on map overload by the time I stopped at the campground entry kiosk. The drawing on the closed window was another map, to the place where I was to register, but when I couldn't even tell which way to turn from the booth, I almost cried in frustration. I breathed deeply. I just needed to find my spot for the night. Across the road and down the hill, I finally found the ranger. He was friendly and apologetic when his credit card receipt printer ate my receipt; I had no reaction at all. I had nothing left. I didn't care. Charge me twice. Don't charge me. It's all the same.

The next day did not begin well. I reached into the dashboard box for my keys so I could listen to the radio while I ate breakfast. Not there. Or anywhere I would expect. I have spares for everything except my ignition key, never anticipating I'd lose it while I was inside Turtle. "Found at last, in a pocket, the last place searched," I wrote in my journal. This last statement only serves to underline the distress of the author. Once the keys are found, why search further? Haha. Old joke.

One day, I'm going to hire myself out to people who write directions to places. I'll test them before publication. The brochure for women's historical spots in Seneca Falls includes where to find Elizabeth Cady Stanton's house in a national park. "Go to Washington Street, turn left. It's on the right."

The house on the corner of Washington Street was a well-tended Victorian, but nothing indicating it was special. Where was the sign acknowledging its historic importance? Well, I was out for a walk anyway, and continued along Washington Street past other tidy old houses. Three blocks further, I found the Stanton house, clearly designated with a big National Park sign and a large parking lot surrounded by a white picket fence. I wondered how many confused feminists had to be redirected by the people in that corner house.

I walked back to the center of town again to look for the Women's Rights National History Park. My brain was refreshed on that crisp fall morning, and it is easier to hunt for things when walking than driving. I didn't have to worry about the pedestrian behind me honking if I stopped to reconnoiter. Some people just have no patience with tourists. The previous day, I'd been given another "drive through town and it's on the left" kind of direction. But nothing about what "it" I was expected to see. I was thinking grass. National Parks have grass, and I only saw old brick buildings and never noticed the actual park that was one of them.

I got sucked into a storefront by an exhibit of Mary Baker Eddy in the window. It had looked promising but turned out to be a Christian Science ruse, posing close to the real museum for innocents like me.

Next to the false exhibit was Declaration Park, the outdoor portion of what I had come to see. All that remains is the skeleton of the church where the historic meeting in 1848 was held. Elizabeth Cady Stanton, Lucretia Mott and three hundred others held the first Women's Rights Convention and began the struggle for women's equality in America. They passed the Declaration of Sentiments and Resolutions, which stated, "Resolved, that it is the duty of the women of this country to secure to themselves their sacred right to the elective franchise." Included in that document was the declaration, "We hold these truths to be self evident; that all men and women are created equal."

Framing the outdoor site is a wide short wall commemorating the women whose names are chiseled in the granite. The sheet of water flowing over the granite reminded me of tears. After more than one hundred fifty years, we still have a long way to go before we have the same opportunities as men. I stood in silence, absorbing the sense of the place, proud that I had been able to make a contribution. While on the board of an association of women's funds, I had worked with the current leaders in women's rights. The work was exhilarating and frustrating and I felt enriched being associated with incredible women every bit as driven as those original activists. Will it ever end?

The real historic park is in the restored two-story brick building behind the weeping wall. The displays were dense with information, and I hope it will go on tour. How many westerners will make it to Seneca Falls?

My favorite part of the exhibit was on the norms of style and how fashion hampered movement and actually made women ill. YES. When I was young, my mother and I never saw eye to eye on what I should be wearing. We still don't. I hated to dress up. I had to wear flimsy dresses and cardboard shoes in high school, when boys got to wear pants and shoes that kept them warm and dry. Most of my freshman year I attended a rural high school where white bucks were quite stylish, those suede oxfords that came with a little bag of white chalk to keep them clean that we all wore with rolled-down socks. And they were comfortable. But mid-year, I transferred back to Lincoln High School in Portland. I continued to wear my white bucks, but was the only girl in school who didn't wear the flimsies. My photo appeared in our local paper when my parents moved a small house down the street to another lot. I gasped when I saw my picture. My feet looked as big as watermelons in those white shoes. So the white bucks went to the back of the closet. I felt more like I belonged at school wearing flimsies, but my feet were always cold. I am envious of girls today who, although still slaves to peer fashion, at least have the option to be physically comfortable.

The museum display of a woman in bloomers riding a bicycle was one of my favorites. Scandalous! I wished I had seen that part of the exhibit when I was much younger to know that when I followed my instincts, I was carrying on a long tradition of rejecting style for comfort. It would have helped me resist caving in to the norms I disliked. And there I was in my hiking boots, shorts and sweaty T-shirt taking it all in

Halfway through the displays, I began to lose interest. Did I really want to be reading about the struggle for equality on that sunny day? I felt the strong urge to hop back in Turtle and go on about the business of being equal. But I stayed and mused on that idea. I get angry whenever I find myself in a beautiful and remote area where I want to just settle in and spend the night. A man could trundle out into the woods and feel free to camp anywhere he pleased. However, I do not. Unless I know an area, I usually spend the night in a state campground or private RV park. When I ask locals, they agree that my precautions are justified. What scares me the most is being alone in an isolated place and having a pickup full of loud and inebriated adolescent boys find me late at night. It has never actually happened but isn't difficult to imagine from the charred remains of beer cans I've found in remote fire rings. I have practiced talking in a very deep voice, for lack of a pair of vicious dogs to protect me. If I am on the other side of my bi-fold door, I hope intruders will believe I'm someone they ought not to mess with. Even in campgrounds, I know my gender is not obvious, and I count on that measure of safety. However, when I march into the "Ladies" restroom, it's a dead give away. It isn't paranoia; only a cautious awareness of a certain level of safety denied me as a woman.

The Women's Rights Park was a sober reminder of the work of so many women that has gone into the freedom that I do enjoy, but we aren't done yet.

September 21, Vermont

In populated areas, where campgrounds are sparse, most RVers know that a Wal Mart parking lot is a safe place to park for the night. In Bennington, Vermont, the local Wal Mart provided a fine accommodation for Turtle and several other rigs. I made a few purchases to justify the use of my spot.

Everyone was still snoozing when I left about 6 a.m. for my morning drive to warm us up before breakfast. In the half-light of dawn I could see a pillar on a hill that looked as if it would have parking and a view. After a few dead ends in a residential area, I found the War Monument, and parked in the empty lot at the base of the decorated pillar. Grand houses surrounded the monument and most windows were dark.

While I assembled breakfast, the sun came up behind me, but to the west, the sky was black. An announcer on the radio read a report of a very bad storm, cars flipped, roofs torn off of two churches. But he only said the he was located in "North Country". The sky was getting blacker, and the wind began, whipping the tops of the trees below me. Was this the storm? Was I in North Country?

I dug out my special radio, which monitors the NOAA (National Oceanic and Atmospheric Administration) weather stations. The report for nearby Albany, New York was for a severe storm warning until 8 a.m. Severe lightning. Heavy hail. High winds. Take cover in a sturdy building, the mechanical voice said. And there I sat, watching the storm approach, parked in the open on the top of a hill.

Where would I be safe? Wal Mart didn't open until eight. Anyway, the windows of another Wal Mart had been blown in already by the storm. I pulled out of the parking lot and passed a police car driving up. Too late, I wondered if I should I have flagged him down. He would have known where I could take cover, but he didn't look as if he was going door to door raising an alarm. In fact, he looked as if he might be on his way to investigate a suspicious vehicle parked at the War Monument.

I drove back through town looking for a sturdy all-night diner. The people in the streets didn't look fussed. Hadn't they heard, or does this happen all the time? I'm such a weather wimp. At home, I'd hear of tornadoes, storms and other weather disasters and thank my stars I live where mudslides, floods and forest fires are our only natural disasters. If it snows, we stay home.

I finally found my diner: Jensen's, open at 7 a.m. for breakfast. The building with large plate-glass windows wasn't quite what I wanted, but it would have to do. I could have parked close to the front door just in case and stayed in Turtle, but if the storm did hit, I might have been blown away in my dash for the building. I felt a bit guilty leaving Turtle to fend for herself, but she was sturdier than I was and would not suffer any pain if injured. Besides, Jensen's had a lovely rest room, something I appreciate in the morning.

The one-egg special with coffee rented the booth and wasn't too filling on top of my first breakfast. The other diners, two singles and a couple, looked quite at home. Regulars, perhaps. I eavesdropped to see if they might be at least aware of the storm, but heard not a peep of concern.

By 8 a.m., the billowy clouds had melted into leaden overcast, except for one to the east. The wind had died, and the rain had almost stopped. I don't think anyone else knew about that particular emergency, but I like to live on the edge.

I wasn't due at the conference until afternoon, so I had plenty of time to enjoy the countryside. Countryside is a misnomer.

Around Sheffield, Massachusetts, I was enjoying the huge yards that surrounded the "country houses." The problem in an area so thickly settled is that there is very little public land, specifically, anyplace with a rest room. What did other people do, the ones in regular cars?

I pulled into a rest stop. Literally a place to rest. In the west, a "rest stop" is a euphemism for a place with rest rooms for humans surrounded by at least a few acres of grass and usually trees, paths to stroll and a coffee trailer run by volunteers hoping for a contribution and a special lawn for dogs. But not here. A rest stop is a place to rest. In fact, the signs at the entrance include an addendum: No Sanitary Facilities.

As I sat on Turtle's biffy, my fertile mind went for a stroll. So, if there were "No Sanitary Facilities", what would I do if I really were in need and didn't have my own on board? Were the unsanitary facilities behind the bushes? Haha. Did I dare even think that thought, here, where every square inch of land is under someone's tight control?

When I settled in my seat with a snack, I looked up. Right in front of me was another strange sign. "Live Parking Only. Unattended Vehicles towed after 30 minutes". Much to think about here.

To my right, under some firs, was a picnic table. So, you can get out of the car. Just don't stay long. However, the symbol for an upcoming picnic table on the highway signs is a tree leaning over a table. In the west, we call leaning trees widow makers, trees that kill. Not much of an incentive to linger. Maybe that's the point.

What is live parking, anyway? Does the car die when everyone leaves? Do the sign makers expect someone to remain inside to keep it alive and attended? Would any body do? Is a dog OK? Does the body have to be alive?

What if I decided to crawl into the back of Turtle and take a nap? Will the thirty-minute monitor creep out of his hiding place, fire up his tow truck and hook me on? What will I do, wedged there between the mattress and the doors, call the driver on my cell phone and explain his error? Will his number be conveniently visible from my rather cramped location for just such emergencies?

It was time to find someone to talk to, and hope they would be tolerant of some senseless babble.

On the final leg to the conference site, I noticed more clearly the intensity of development I was seeing. Given my preference for undeveloped areas, it is no wonder I felt cramped. At home, infill development is being encouraged to increase the density of housing, covering over our garden plots for another condo. Imagine that sort of movement occurred every fifty years, as it probably did there in Massachusetts. More houses, more shops, open spaces shrink except for those settled years before and being held intact against the encroaching development. This is the result. Every square inch under control, built on, or preserved, defended by some "Friends of" group so the kids would know a trail, a wild bird or rabbit.

September 26, Maine

The conference was a nice break, but it felt good to get back on the road. I had directions to the house of some friends I'd met on a rafting trip, in southern New Hampshire, but the back roads I drove braid the countryside like the rivulets on a river delta. It is a challenge for the people who number the roads and those who drive them. One road had been assigned four different numbers, some headed east, some south and sometimes both south and north. No wonder I got lost and had to call for new directions from 100 miles southeast of their home. I was late for dinner, but they were gracious.

Having a firm destination cramps my freewheeling schedule. My more social friends are aghast when I say things like that, but we all have our priorities. If I hadn't been expected, I wouldn't have been lost.

One of the goals for my trips was to see a moose. When I mentioned it to Julia, a friend I saw at the conference, she described seeing a moose on her property on the coast of Maine and invited me to stop over. The chance to see a moose was worth being lost again if I missed another turn.

There are no moose in Oregon, but when I was young, my mother's brother, my Uncle Ralph, showed us a very old home movie my Grandfather Smith had taken when the two of them went hunting in Canada. Ralph's narrative highlighted his father's reaction when he could not find Ralph one afternoon. Ralph was around twelve at the time. He had gotten bored with the hunting chatter between his father and the guides and wandered off. When his father saw an empty canoe out on the lake, he panicked and sent all the guides out to look for Ralph's floating body. They found Ralph lying peacefully on the bottom of the canoe watching the clouds. Ralph was annoyed at the disruption but his father was livid at the panic he had felt when he discovered Ralph's absence. The wash of relief one might expect in a father who had just found his only son alive and well in such a situation was not part of my grandfather's personality. He was used to being in tight control of everyone around him, and that included his son. At the time, he still had the false notion that Ralph would follow him into business, so it was the guides that got the tongue-lashing.

While Ralph laughed as he recalled his father's fury at the guides for their inattention, grainy scenes of trails and portages flickered onto the screen. Men stood in front of a log cabin, posing in their high-laced boots, heavy pants and jackets. Then, we saw a moose swimming the lake, just its head and huge rack of antlers visible in the stuttering picture. After some checkered frames, which indicated the camera had been turned off and on, the moose emerged from some willows, munching a mouthful of twigs and branches, water gushing from its thick hair. Even with little for comparison, I could tell it was enormous. The moose was apparently uninterested in the cameraman, who held steady while the moose stared, which may have left me with a false sense of security in the presence of such a beast.

My uncle's story was a family legend, but what remained vivid in my memory was that moose emerging from the willows. I wanted to see a wild moose.

On a walk near her house, Julia pointed out moose prints in the dust at the side of the road.

"Oh, yes," she said, "A family of moose come through the yard but we usually only see their hoof prints. I've only seen one once. It was just standing in that marsh, looking at me," she said, pointing across a small wetland, "but they hide during the day. Sometimes the dogs bark into the brush, and I know one is in there somewhere, but I've never seen one when it wants to be hidden."

Hot dog. Tonight, I will see a moose. I could feel it.

When I retired to Turtle after a sumptuous dinner cooked by Julia's husband, I vowed to peek under the back curtain every time I woke up. I was a light sleeper, and now that I was on a quest, I would sleep even lighter. Turtle was parked right in the gravel drive, so the moose had to pass nearby.

The moon was late in rising. I fell into a light sleep and awoke with an uncertain feeling that I had heard something. A huff, or grunt, but I wasn't sure. Then I heard it again. A snort. I looked out the back and saw a solid black something with short horizontal white lines on both sides. My brain tried to make sense of what I was seeing when the black shadow floated to the left, leaving an unbroken white line, which turned out to be a long plastic sheet stretched along the drive, a remnant of some new construction.

That shadow had to be my moose! I jumped to the front window to scan the drive where it had to be headed. No moose. I averted my eyes, hoping the rods on my retina would pick up any soft shadow. Nothing. My tiny flashlight didn't help, barely reaching five feet into the thick black. What to do. Race outside for a better look? The air was brisk and I was naked. By the time I got dressed, the moose would be even further away. If I did brave the cold, with my luck, the door would slam behind me and lock, leaving me in my lily white skin radiating all my bed-heat into the night, having to knock on Julia's door for rescue and what if her husband answered the door . . . Never mind. I'd have to wait for another moose.

I dived back into my warm nest, fully awake. What just happened? Lucky for the white plastic stretched along the drive or I might never have noticed the shadow against such a dark background. And if it was a moose, what went on in a huge animal's mind as it huffed at Turtle's white and unmoving form? Maybe it was challenging Turtle for possession of the driveway. It must have known that even at two thousand pounds, it was no match for Turtle's dainty bulk.

In the morning, I looked for tracks. Maybe I found some, blurred, but were they from my moose, or one that passed through earlier? Alas. I'd never know.

September 27, Maine

As Julia prepared for a busy day, I called my friend, Anita, in Guysborough, Nova Scotia to let her know I was getting close. I'd told her before I left home that I might show up sometime around the end of September, but had made no commitment. I was so close it seemed silly not to go that last leg east for a visit since I hadn't seen her in many years. She told me that the next day was her day off. I had wanted to dawdle a bit along the coast of New Brunswick and Nova Scotia, but I let that plan go so I could spend more time with her. Choices, choices.

After a fast but scenic drive along the rugged New Brunswick coast and into Nova Scotia, I realized I would not make Guysborough that night so when I saw the sign to Pugwash, I knew I had to detour. When I lived in Vancouver, British Columbia I had noted a reference to Pugwash in the news. A whole movement was spawned from a private gathering that took place in 1957 at the Pugwash mansion of Cyrus Eaton, an industrialist and philanthropist. He was an advocate for nuclear disarmament and gathered scientists for the first Conference on Science and World Affairs. The annual Pugwash Conference has continued to meet around the world to discuss ways to temper the arms race and examine the social responsibility of scientists in such areas as economic development, population growth and environmental destruction. The conference received a Nobel Prize in 1995 for the work. And it all started in this little town on the northern coast of Nova Scotia. What a strange name to immortalize, but Canadians never seemed to worry about such things.

In the few hours of daylight left I drove toward Pugwash on a country road bordered by small fenced pastures supporting a few sheep and cows. At the coast, I turned east into the town. Seaside residents of the small village have gorgeous ocean views across rocky beaches and the Northumberland Strait toward Prince Edward Island. Most houses were small and practical, not the sumptuous vacation homes I have come to expect in such a spectacular place. Hefty fishing boats filled the marina, rugged work craft for making a living off the sea. Directions to the famous Pugwash mansion did not jump out at me, and it was time to think about finding a place for the night. Seeing the town was enough for the moment.

The only campground listed in my book was prematurely closed for the season, but I knew the Nova Scotians were a peaceful people. Near Malagash, I parked on a muddy and deserted lot next to an intersection with only one house across the road. Traffic was light and no one bothered me. Anita told me later if I hadn't moved after three days, maybe, someone would have knocked to see if I was all right. That would be the extent of any invasion.

The next morning, I got an early start, anxious to see Anita again. She is one of two doctors in Guysborough, a village in the southeast corner of Nova Scotia. We first met when we were volunteer teachers in Tanzania in the 1960's. She taught homemaking and I taught all the sciences at Bwiru Girls Secondary School. When Anita returned to Canada, she finished her medical degree in family practice and has been the doctor in the Guysborough area ever since. I visited a few times when I lived in Canada, but hadn't seen her for twenty years.

Anita had told me she would be at the hospital until about 10 a.m. I found the small hospital and long-term care center on a point of land at the edge of town. Her hospital serves the surrounding rural area of about 3500 souls, as Anita puts it. Even on her day off, she has to do rounds and I found her in her final conference with the staff. She hadn't changed much in twenty years, the same dark, curly hair and hurried, choppy forward-tilted gait. Anita isn't a public hugger, but she called out, "Harriet. Glad you found me." Same accent, broadening some vowels and skipping over others. She introduced me to the people around her like family. Their manner was casual but respectful; they joked easily, and deferred comfortably to Doctor Foley.

I followed her home for a cup of tea and her cigarette. I was dismayed to see she still smoked, something I would avoid now in a new acquaintance. Anita was ready for a drive in the country, which she enjoys but rarely does. She thought I might be interested in looking for migrating sandpipers in the bays. Oh, goody. More driving. But with Anita at the wheel, I could watch the scenery, and we had a great time catching up as we wandered around the inlets, coves, points of land and islands. The day was warm in the weakening fall sun, but crisp in the shade, and the slight breeze called for a jacket when we got out to enjoy the views.

Guysborough is located at the head of the Chedabucto Bay, the deep bay cut into the southeast corner of the Nova Scotia mainland. We drove down the Canso Peninsula, southeast of Guysborough and pulled off at a viewpoint where we could see the other side of the bay, and beyond that, Cape Breton Island. Then we looped south to Tor Bay and poked into inlets looking for the thousands of sand pipers reported to be passing. They must have passed already, because we never found them. It didn't matter.

Anita was a great tour guide. "The rocky soil is not good for commercial agriculture and the stumpy pine, spruce and hemlock trees have been logged many times, and provide only wood chips and firewood so most of the people depend on the land and sea to survive. I've seen most of them at some time as patients. I always have lots of fresh seafood during the season. They bring me fresh fish, scallops and lobsters and one old codger even brings sea water so I can cook the lobster properly."

Anita pointed to one of the tiny house perched on the rocky shore. "Old Jack lives there. He's a character," Anita said, laughing.

"I was called out one winter night when he came in with a possible heart attack. After he undressed for a complete exam, the nurse called me in, whispering, 'You're not going to believe this.'"

"When I entered the examining room, I saw that his feet were black with dirt. "Jack," I exclaimed, "Your feet are filthy!"

"Jack looked down, and said, "Well, Doc, the harbor is frozen over so how could I clean them?""

We stopped at a little general store for a snack. "Hi, Kathleen. How're you doing?"

"Oh, just fine, Doc."

"Good. How's Joe? Feelin' OK, now?"

"Oh, yes, thank you. Fit as a fiddle. I'm glad you came by. I was going to come into town this afternoon and bring you some cranberries we picked this morning. You saved me the trip."

The woman stooped to grab a heavy plastic bag from behind the counter and handed it to Anita. It held a gallon of the tiny wild cranberries that were ripening along the roads and on the nearby public lands. Good for jellies, Anita said.

We picked out a snack to stave off hunger until lunch, and Anita pulled out her wallet.

"Naw. It's on the house, Doc."

"Nope, Kathleen. Can't let you do that. You're too generous, and you can't make a living that way. The cranberries are plenty and I thank you for them."

I watched Kathleen make the change. She had the same easy familiarity mixed with respect for Anita as the nurses at the hospital did.

We drove past a tip of land near Goldboro to the south where a wide and treeless corridor gashed the forest. A gas pipeline from Sable Island, located about 100 miles offshore, had been recently buried deep in the ground there where it first touched land on its way to the new gas plant. Anita had not seen the plant yet, so we turned onto the access road to investigate. It looked like what it was, a big gas plant with lots of huge green pipes winding among the tanks. The builders had promised it would attract businesses that could benefit from cheap gas, but at that point, only trees surrounded it. Time will tell.

"It's been rather controversial out there among the pines and cranberries. The gas is processed here before being sent on down the pipe to New England. Halifax hadn't paid much attention to this corner of the province for years. Then they discovered how much money the local government was getting from the gas plant. Now they want their share," Anita said.

Some things are universal.

Sky blue, yellow or occasionally pink houses stood out gaily against the dark trees and rocks in the area around Larry's River. We made a big loop to the southwest to get back to Guysborough.

"You can always tell where the Acadians live. They pretty much stick together and they love bright colors. They're the descendants of French settlers, and are among the poorest inhabitants of the province, but they add such a rich texture to the area. Any time we have some community celebration, they come with crafts and music to liven things up."

On a visit to New Orleans, I'd enjoyed the Cajun food, music and spirit. Cajuns in Louisiana are the descendants of Acadians who were forced to leave Nova Scotia in the mid-eighteenth century. Back then, the hundred extended French families had lived in Nova Scotia long enough to form their own culture and they had remained neutral in the territorial disputes between the British and the French. As the hostilities increased, the British could not trust the neutrality of the Acadians and demanded they swear allegiance to the British Crown. Most refused, so in 1755, the British Governor Charles Lawrence ordered them all to leave, sending 8,000 Acadians to the 13 English colonies and Europe during the infamous Acadian Expulsion. Later, they were allowed to return, but their rich farm lands had been taken by other settlers. They were not allowed to settle in numbers large enough to form self-sufficient colonies and they gradually have settled along the remote coastal regions of the province like the Guysborough area.

Driving back to Guysborough, Anita remembered another patient who she told to use Polysporin, an antibiotic ointment, on the abrasions he'd gotten from a fall. A few days later, Anita saw the town's pharmacist on the street who waved her down for a chat. He had found the fellow wandering around the drug store, looking a bit confused.

"Can I help you, Ned," he'd asked.

"Well, John, Doc Foley told me to get some stuff for these cuts here, but I can't find anything that looks right."

"Well, what are you looking for? Maybe I can help you."

"Doc told me to get some polyester and smear it on good but I don't see anything like that on the shelves here," he said.

Anita went on, "Another patient, an older lady, came in to see about a pain in her lower abdomen and frequency of urination, although she didn't phrase it like that. After an examination and some tests, I tried to be discreet with the old dear, so I told her she had a little problem with her water and needed some tablets. I wrote her a prescription for her urinary infection and gave it to her. She nodded and left.

"She took the paper home and pumped her well dry. Then, she put the tablets down the well with the Javex, which we use to clean our wells when we drain them." Anita laughed with delight.

Another person telling the same stories might seem to be making fun of the patients, but Anita was clearly fond of every person, and related each anecdote like I might tell stories on a well loved and eccentric relative. Clearly, she was well suited to her practice.

Anita and I made it back to Guysborough for a late lunch of a thick soup and whole wheat bread at a new bakery. Over lunch, Anita told me a bit more about her community.

Giovanni Caboto, John Cabot, was commissioned by Henry VII of England to discover unknown land. He arrived at Cape Breton Island on June 24, 1497 and possibly visited the Guysborough area on his second and last trip in 1498. The French established a fort at the mouth of the harbor in 1654. The village carried on extensive trade with Europe and the New England colonies in its heyday. Cattle, sheep, fish and timber were shipped out of the very busy harbor from the rich farmlands inland. When rail lines were laid to the center of the province, Guysborough gradually faded. The nearby fishing grounds were over fished for years by ships from many nations, and the loss of the fishery in the last twenty years has been devastating to local fishermen. Guysborough is still the service center for a county population of 9000, as the seat of the municipal government. That's half the population of a hundred years ago.

Recently, wealthy German families have bought up waterfront land around Guysborough and have built large summer houses after their second homes on the Adriatic became part of a war zone. Most of the families stay to themselves during the time they visit and are not a part of the community.

As Anita paid the bill, she and the owners of the bakery grumbled about the proposed installation of sidewalks, due to happen in the next months. Recently, a few leisure visitors have been finding Guysborough, and one entrepreneur is building a rather large market between the main street and the bay, with tourists in mind. But tourists will mean increased traffic and changes, including a rather dramatic alteration of the casual parking arrangements currently in use. Now, people just drive up onto the muddy shoulder and point their vehicles at the store they intend to visit. After the sidewalks are installed, only parallel parking will be allowed and will accommodate fewer vehicles. Where will all the tourists park, they wondered, though I thought the more relevant question had to do with where they would park their own cars.

A newly arrived German couple had opened an upscale restaurant in one of the old houses on the hill in town and we joined Elizabeth, the other Guysborough doctor, for dinner there one evening. Only seven patrons sat in the tiny dining area, but the food was excellent.

Anita and Elizabeth alternated nights and weekends on call. A hard schedule, but Anita was used to it. Unfortunately, Elizabeth was preparing to leave, and Anita would again be the only doctor. When she started her practice in Guysborough thirty years ago, she shared it with her sister, but since she left, Anita has often been the only doctor. As she nears retirement age, she and the people of the town worry about the future.

Anita laughed at the inconveniences of being on call all the time, but the pay is good for the extra work. Though single, Anita's large and close-knit family lives around Antigonish, an hour's drive to the north, and she's been generous in helping her nieces and nephews get off to a good start in life. Her bridge partners are used to disrupted games, and on many nights she isn't called at all. In my opinion, she earns whatever she gets.

Anita can't walk around town because she might be paged to the hospital at the edge of town at any moment. People know her red SUV and always know where the doc is. Patients stop her on the street with their complaints, though Anita tries to get them to make an office visit. Street side diagnosis is difficult even for the best of doctors.

I spent the night in Anita's guest room, contrary to my policy of sleeping in Turtle even when offered a bed in the house of a host. I tell them that Turtle is my home, and my bed is right there. I don't know why I made an exception at Anita's but I must have made ten trips out to get things I had forgotten to bring inside. The next night I spent in Turtle and worried about what I had left inside.

My second day in Guysborough was a working day for Anita, so I puttered. It was nice to have a low-key day. The weather was threatening rain, but the prototype brochure for tourist attractions Anita gave me showed a walking/bicycling path that skirted the town. I hauled out my bicycle and gave it a try. The path was not well posted and it wandered up brushy side roads and driveways. After the first ten minutes, I was never certain if I was really on the official path, though whatever path I was on was pleasant. The tourism department has a little work to do.

I told Anita at lunch that I planned a walk along the shore and she warned me that the German owner of one house was not too friendly. The family had made it known that townspeople were not welcome to walk in front of their property where they had always walked. I did anyway, banking on being a tourist and pleading ignorance, but the house seemed unoccupied. Around the tip of the peninsula, the rocky shore petered out into yards and brush, so I ended up crashing through bushes to regain the road back to town, typical of many of my hikes.

Anita fixed scallops for dinner, last season's frozen gift. Anita's other houseguest joined us. She was a young woman in town to rehearse a part in a play that was to open soon. Guysborough has no hotel, and Anita often has short-term guests like her who come and go on their own schedule. The actor seemed tired that night but she was a good audience for Anita and me as we recalled some of our experiences in Africa.

"This seafood reminds me of the time you walked into your classroom and smelled fish."

"Oh, yes," Anita laughed. "The mayflies were flying in thick clouds from Lake Victoria, dying in heaps under the outdoor lights. They were mostly air, fluffy like a pile of down feathers, no weight or substance. The girls had gathered enough to make a few tiny patties, which they were baking in my ovens. They had a very strong fishy smell, probably from what they were eating, and they looked very greasy. I declined the treat, but I let the girls finish their snack before class."

My influence on the bakers was less tasty. In one of my biology classes, I mentioned that if you were really starving, lichens were a source of nutrition. I think what I had read about was the

Old Man's Beard type of lichen that hangs from swamp trees, but some of the girls wanted to test the theory. They scraped the crusty gray-green lichen off the rocks and baked it up in a tiny loaf of bread. Four of them came down to my house one afternoon, giggling and elbowing each other. They wanted me to try their survival bread. I did, but it tasted like a rock, and was about as tender. We all agreed we would have to be really starving before it would be worth eating.

My last night in Guysborough, very low temperatures had been predicted and I got warm in the house and jumped right into my nest in Turtle to transfer the heat quickly. Only the first moment was a shock and soon I was comfy. The temperature dropped below freezing that night for the first time on the trip and with my two-quilt combo I was quite toasty.

Frost covered the windshield at 6 a.m. Anita had persuaded me to stay until daylight so she could say goodbye. When I saw the hall light go on, I joined her for toast and coffee and a nice chat. By 7:30 she was eying her Saturday New York Times crossword. Anita is a person of habit, guest or not, so it seemed like a good time to depart.

Anita is one of the people in my life who is a friend because of a quirk of time. We spent two years together, building a history and enjoying each other's company where there were few choices for companionship among the eight to twelve teachers at our school. Not being a people person, it's the long history of shared experience that ripens my friendships. Passing acquaintances don't stand a chance. In spite of lives that have diverged, we still share a certain sense of humor and a quirky way of seeing things.

September 30, Nova Scotia

I had a ticket to sail from Digby to St. John, New Brunswick in a day and a half so I had a bit of time to explore. The weather was still sunny, but windy and cold. Many of the little towns seemed to be closed down for the season already. I had to keep in mind the Elderhostel course I had registered for in Provincetown on Cape Cod started on October 8th, and I wanted to see the fall colors in New England before it began so I didn't try to explore the southern coast of Nova Scotia.

I did chance onto Shubenacadie Wildlife Park, named after a local tribe. I put on some extra layers to cope with the chilly wind and paid my fee. In a pen at the back of the park, a sedate moose lay in some grass and chewed his cud. Even from a distance, I marveled at its rack of antlers. How could that enormous animal hide so well as Julia said they did? OK, this was a moose. But he wasn't in the wild. He wasn't even standing up. Close, but no cigar.

I found a resident bar headed goose among some wild Canada geese that had dropped in for a snack in one of the pens. A native of India and Nepal, it is found only in private collections and zoos in North America. The goose was bit smaller than the visitors, with a silvery gray back, white neck stripe and black bars across its white head.

On a side trail, I happened on a well-shaded pond where three stunning mandarin ducks paddled. They are also Asian natives, closely related to wood ducks, and have a glossy purple chest, tawny body and a white eye stripe above very fine golden feathers that give the impression of a man's pork chop sideburns.

I have difficulty comprehending that creatures like those ducks are real and not a product of someone's vivid imagination. I was careful not to call attention to my find for fear the crowd of school kids racing around the other pathways would disturb their serenity.

The rest of the day I spent on road detours.

My night's stop was Dunromin' Camp Ground, one of the seedier ones I used. I was assigned an uneven site next to an unoccupied algae-flecked trailer covered with flapping black plastic. No pad or graveled area. In fact, the site was just a post with a number and an electrical box on it in a grassy field. The weak sun was sinking by the time I settled in and a cold wind blew through a row of evergreens that separated my site from the Annapolis River.

Anita had sent me away with some of the bread and a big bag of homegrown tomatoes that had been left on her car seat by a patient. I had bought some freshly picked apples and ginger cookies at a roadside stand. They made a great dinner. As I ate, I worried that the ferry ride would be rough if the wind didn't calm down. I don't like feeling seasick.

Turtle had warmed up nicely by the time I stopped for breakfast. Out my windshield, I could see the town of Annapolis Royal to the left and low hills on either side of the long, skinny body of water that formed a well-protected harbor for fisheries. k.d. lang sang for my breakfast. On the news, the Olympic games in Sydney, Australia had just finished and Canadians were lining up in Ottawa to say sad goodbyes to Pierre Trudeau, who was Prime Minister during the time I lived in Canada.

I was parked in the visitor parking for Annapolis Royal Tidal Generating Station, the first and only saltwater tidal power plant in North America. It was built in 1984 as a pilot project where the 23-foot Bay of Fundy tides generate 30 million kilowatt-hours of electricity each year. When I was in school, the amazingly high tides in the Bay had caught my attention. I had wanted to see the tidal bore, the wall of water that rushed in with every incoming tide, a phenomena due to the tidal range of over fifty feet. At one time, the tidal bore at Moncton, New Brunswick, on the other side of the Bay of Fundy was ten feet high. On a previous visit I'd made a special trip to Moncton to see the bore race up the Petitcodiac River. What a disappointment to learn that construction at the mouth of the river had diminished the bore to only two feet high. Still, it was startling to see the perpendicular knee-high wall of water swish and hiss its way up the river, quickly covering the muddy riverbed in front of me.

Tides almost as extreme do occur in other places in the world. Years before on the coast of western Canada, my husband and I beached our canoe for the night at high tide and had to walk it and the all our gear out more than half a mile the next morning. The shape of the bottom of the sea and the shore determine whether the bore occurs, and the Bay of Fundy has it all. People from all over the world wait at the viewing areas around the Bay of Fundy as I had done to watch the tidal bores. It made good sense to harness some of that energy.

The generator for the plant was inside the dam next to where I was parked. The incoming tide fills the catch basin on the upriver side of the dam. At the peak of the tide, the sluice gates close. When the level of the outgoing tide is five feet below the level of water in the catch basin, the gates open and the water flows through the massive generator to produce a peak of 20 megawatts of power for about five hours. The plant generates about 1% of Nova Scotia's electrical power capacity.

I love seeing how people have used local resources to resolve local needs. In a period when power supplies are hot political topics, this solution seems so obvious and so economical and has none of the problems of long-distance transmission.

I like to try small fast food places; I have some bizarre notion about sharing that experience with the locals, though at home I am never one of the locals in those places. On my way to Digby, I had the "Tim Horton" fast food experience. This chain sells baked goods and I was thinking of a glazed doughnut when I walked in the door. I read somewhere that glazed doughnuts weren't too bad for me as doughnuts go. Or maybe I only thought I read it, as I do, creating my own favorable culinary news to support my sugar habit. In line, I got into a conversation with a well-dressed French Canadian woman who recommended the Chocolate Boston Cream. To honor her tip, I ordered one. She didn't stick around for my reaction since she was buying something for her drive into Halifax. The confection was OK until I hit the gooey thick filling made with lots of cornstarch. With the sweet chocolate icing on top, it was way too much chocolate for me. A friend told me later that French Canadians love really sweets. Now I know to be suspicious of their advice. So much for Tim Horton.

I lived on a wooden schooner for a year and am drawn to walk the docks of marinas. In Digby, pulled my jacket tight against the wind and walked out along the commercial wharf that hooked into the bay to see what might be going on that Sunday morning. A few seagulls joined me, but no boats were unloading the fish or scallops that give this town life, so there wasn't much to interest them. The tide was low and the boats bobbed fifteen to twenty feet below the level of the wharf, a good example of the effect and possible problems of the extreme tides. Only the tops of the masts and the ends of the booms were visible until I peered over the side to find the tough little fishing boats rocking gently in the lee of the wharf. Their scoured decks were ready for the next trip, but the crews had taken the day off. I tried to imagine the added work involved in loading and unloading supplies and catch with that much of a drop to the deck. I noticed a few small cranes on the wharf, which must have helped.

About noon, I pulled into the priority boarding line at the Digby Ferry dock. Vehicles of all sorts surrounded me with licenses from New York, Louisiana, Massachusetts but not many from Maine, the closest state. A couple of young women had a map spread on the hood of their car, pointing and discussing their next move in German. A guy driving a truck tractor unloaded a number of empty trailers from the recently arrived ferry and parked them alongside other trailers full of wood chips lined up at the edge of the parking area. Those chips are what is left of the once thriving lumber industry.

Lumber production was an important industry early in the history of Nova Scotia. By 1871 there were reportedly 1144 sawmills operating, mostly water powered. Oak and elm planks, beams and rafters filled the cargo holds bound for France. According to Elizabeth May, in *At the Cutting Edge*, Nova Scotia now has probably the most intensively harvested forest in Canada but the practice of taking only the best trees has left a depleted genetic stock. Most of the forestland is in private hands, the bulk of it owned by American and European paper companies so even the hardwoods are chipped and shipped to foreign paper mills.

What I noticed on the highways were log trucks with eight-foot-long logs loaded crosswise, probably headed for chippers. Around Guysborough, each eight-inch diameter tree yielded only one of those lengths. Not only is genetics a problem, but after centuries growing trees and harvesting them from rocky ground, any nourishment left is inadequate to grow the forests that once flourished on that land. At home, the clear cutting debate is dying down as scientists discover that it is possible to harvest good timber without destroying the whole forest, but sustainable yield logging hasn't been fully implemented. Tree farms cut their trees after forty to seventy years, and we have only raised two or three "crops" since the old growth was first felled. How long can we do that before the soil can only support the growth of trees the size of these puny ones, where they have been cut for several hundred years, even if we leave hardy stock for replenishment?

When it was my turn to load, I drove slowly in line down the ramp and into the dark auto deck, following the signals of the men waving us down one alley or another. After we were loaded, the tractor started up again, filling the spaces with the full chip trailers. A tinny voice directed passengers to move to the passenger decks. I considered staying below for a nap, as I have on ferry trips in the northwest, but I wanted to watch the Nova Scotia shore slide by, so I joined the other passengers in the comfortable lounge.

The ferry's motor was so smooth I never felt us leave the dock. Ferry food is not noted for its quality but I wandered into the cafeteria just to see what was being offered. A glance at the menu convinced me I had to try a scallop burger. I imagined little round scallop meats arranged around a bun. Would there be one in the center, surrounded by six or eight others? Or four or five in a tight circle? When I pried the top off my bun I found one patty of ground meat. It looked like any other burger, only a little lighter in color. Well, of course. Think of the time it would take to arrange those little round meats on that bun. A patty is so much easier to manipulate. It was tasty but the bun was dry.

After moseying around the windy outer deck and watching the harbor fade into the distance, I found a lovely warm spot on the aft deck. It was next to an ashtray, I discovered, after I had plunked myself down, and another woman huddled close by with her hood up over her head, smoking.

A large man in a white shirt with gold braid on the shoulders sat down between us.

He smiled at me and said, "Sorry for smoking right here, but this is where even the crew has to come if we want to smoke." He was chatty. Six years to retirement. "The company was sold not long ago to a private company and cut the crew in half. Now, I have to live on board for six days at a time. Don't get much time to see my family." He seemed tired and sad and lonesome, I'd say.

He filled me in on ferry activities. The reason for reservations is that cars and RVs get first priority, trucks second and chip trailers third. A late RV with no reservation might not get on if the trucks and chip trailers had filled the space already. There's a LOT of truck traffic, he said. The Digby ferry carries most of the trucks that haul products in and out of Nova Scotia. The officer said the 5 a.m. sailing takes the bulk of the commercial traffic and helps them catch up with trucks and chippers. I had considered taking that sailing after spending the night at the dock, but there would have been a lot of heavy motors going all night, so I'm glad I didn't.

He got to the subject of rough weather. "We don't often cancel a sailing but it can get pretty rough out there. They tie the trucks down and chock the tires, but they can still break loose. One time, we had a potato truck tip over. Potatoes rolled all over the deck. It was a mess.

"And if someone forgets to turn off the propane in their motor home, that rocking can start a fire. You don't want to be down there if we have a fire. Sometimes we can get it out with foam, but if we can't, we have to flood the whole deck with a fire suppressant. Don't know what it is. Carbon dioxide, maybe. But everyone has to be out before they pull the switch and hope no one is in their vehicle."

Something to think about next time I'm tempted to take a nap rather than join the rest of the passengers in the lounge.

October 2, New Brunswick

Campobello, the summer retreat of Franklin D. Roosevelt, was just down the road from my campground. I read the description in my guidebook and wondered how Roosevelt got there from Washington, D.C. How had he managed the country that far from the capitol? The campground hostess did not know the answers to my questions, but convinced me it was worth the trip to visit. They always took their guests there.

I had to drive down the coast for an hour in the U.S. and then re-enter Canada at the little customs station in Lubec, Maine, the first town in the United States to see the sunrise their signs bragged. I crossed the bridge and followed the directions to Campobello International Park, a cooperative project of the US and Canadian governments. From the empty parking lot, I could see the large saltbox cottage where Franklin Roosevelt and his family spent so many summers. The recently built visitor's center didn't open until 10, so I had time for a hike.

The first section of a trail marked "Friar's Bay" passed through an old apple orchard, trunks and limbs rough with lichen. The tang of fermenting apples filled the air but there was no sign of the deer I would have expected, resourceful foragers. A few fall asters lingered in the meadow at the base of the headland and after half an hour, I was at the viewing platform looking north into Friar's Bay.

As the mid-morning sun worked on the fog, I was able to pick out a dozen weirs poking out of the bay, lines of sticks set up to catch fish as the tide receded. Across the water lay Eastport, Maine where fingers of land protect the harbor. A sign on the railing pointed out the mouth of beautiful Cobscook Bay and the remains of an unfinished tidal generator in one of the passes between the islands. When it was built years ago, it was not the exotic source of energy it would be today. No information on why it wasn't finished. Maybe they will reconsider.

Back at the visitor's center, the first tour bus had arrived, but the passengers were in the cottage and I had the exhibits to myself. I scoured them for answers to my questions about the role Campobello played while Roosevelt was president and discovered answers to questions I hadn't even asked. Standing there in the visitor's center with photos, drawings, charts and narrative, it was all interesting.

In 1881, the island was sold to a group of entrepreneurs who were developing it as a summer retreat for the wealthy families of Boston, New York and Montreal. The Roosevelt family first visited in 1883 when Franklin was one year old and they purchased their lot where they built a fifteen-room cottage.

I choke on the term they use for such a large house. My kind of cottage is small, maybe with a little porch, two or three rooms and that's it. This one, large as it was, had no electricity or phone. People like the Roosevelts, who liked fireplace heat on the foggy days, and cranky kerosene lamps, were called rusticators, those who enjoyed the rustic life. I liked that. I would have fit right in.

After Franklin's marriage to Eleanor, the couple lived with Franklin's widowed mother, Sara, when on the island. The house I was visiting originally belonged to Mrs. Hartman Kuhn who was the next-door neighbor. She and Eleanor became good friends, and when she died, she had stipulated in her will that Sara could buy her 34-room house provided she gave it to Franklin and Eleanor. She understood the pressures on Eleanor by Sara, who was a domineering mother-in-law.

Painted barn red and white, the cottage was shaped like a barn, and inside, felt like a beach house, simple and rugged. The many rooms accommodated Roosevelt's large family and frequent guests, and I noted that the servant's rooms were not much smaller than the ones the children had. I hoped it showed a respect for the people who worked for them.

The trip to Campobello for the Roosevelts took three-days and four trains from their home in New York to Eastport, Maine. There they were met by a carriage and taken to a boat for the last leg to Campobello. Franklin was less able to vacation on the island once he began his political career, leaving Eleanor and the children to enjoy it without his dynamic presence. As Assistant Secretary of the Navy, Roosevelt used his position to order the battleship USS North Dakota to Eastport and it was Roosevelt himself who guided the ship through the treacherous waters to port.

In 1921, after a failed run for vice-president, Franklin was able to manage a short visit to Campobello. It was on that trip that he was struck by polio. Louis Howe, a close friend, said it is possible that Franklin's limited mobility forced him to focus his energy and enabled him to attain the presidency he had set as a personal goal even as a young man.

While Franklin was president, the Roosevelts were unable to visit Campobello for several years. After President Roosevelt's death, Eleanor bought the property from the estate for her son Elliot for $1000 and was able to visit only three more times. The houses fell into disrepair and in 1952, Elliot sold the property to Armand Hammer who restored the cottage and installed electricity and a telephone. Unable to sell it years later, he donated it for the park. In 1962, President John F. Kennedy proposed a Campobello Park as a memorial to Franklin D. Roosevelt

As I wandered the grounds, I appreciated the restoration, having undertaken a similar project years ago. Inside, the downstairs rooms were furnished as they had been, looking ready for the family to arrive. Upstairs, I stood in the hallway, able to see into several of the children's bedrooms, and imagined I could hear the gleeful shouts and thunder of feet on the wooden stairs. The sailing, hiking and clamming they did would have suited me fine. Even the cool days when the fog settled in would mean fires in the fireplaces and quiet reading.

Down the road, I stopped at Lupine Lodge, built when logs were cheap and sawmills scarce. I had to roust out the staff for some food, and the service was slow. They weren't serving many customers at 11 a.m., but it was time for my breakfast. A 5-pronged moose head watched me from the log wall, and a huge stone fireplace with enormous andirons, open on both sides, filled the center of the dining room. The lodge would have been wonderful on a chillier day, a place to pause in front of a roaring fire, but that day the hearth was cold.

I was the only food customer, but four local women were having coffee and a lively chat at a table behind the fireplace. They were island entrepreneurs, with small, service-oriented companies. I could only catch snippets of their conversation. One had to leave soon to blow up balloons to supply an upcoming event. They covered investments and mortgage rates, local marriages, babies and divorces and between the serious stuff they joked and roared with laughter at themselves. Their comfortable conversation made me feel a bit lonesome for a chat with a few good friends.

As I ate, the staff bustled around setting up for a large number of people for lunch, probably the tour bus. When I was done, I left the rest of my Canadian money as a tip and said goodbye to Canada.

Julia had told me to be sure to visit the bicycle paths in Acadia National Park on the south coast of Maine. The portion I visited is the most developed and the oldest part of the park, located on Mount Desert Island. In the early eighteenth century, the inhabitants were engaged in fishing, shipbuilding, lumbering or farming, but by mid-century, artists, sportsmen and journalists had discovered the unspoiled wilderness. These new tourists stayed with the local families, who called them summercators. By 1880, Bar Harbor had 30 hotels and the wealthy industrialists like the Rockefellers, Fords and Astors had begun to build their summer cottages on the island. The mansions and supporting infrastructure changed the previously rustic nature of the island forever. Paradoxically, those same people were instrumental in preserving the natural beauty of the island.

In 1913 John D. Rockefeller, Jr. responded to the threat of increasing automobile traffic by initiating the development of the 57 miles of gravel carriage roads that are now available for hiking and biking. Steeper trails offer hikers and bikers a more vigorous workout. I chose the relatively flat carriage road and as I pedaled, I tried to imagine the creak of leather and clop of hooves of horse drawn carriages on the same tree-lined paths a century ago. The weather was perfect, a bit cool so I could work off some steam but not build up a dripping sweat. I only encountered a few people on my hour's ride and no carriages since the carriage rentals were closed for winter.

After a good ride, I loaded up my bike and joined the line of cars headed for the top of Cadillac Mountain to see the "awesome 360 degree view of the ocean, islands, jagged coastline and woods and lakes" of Mount Desert Island and the surrounding islands, according to the park brochure. The traffic moved so slowly, I abandoned that idea, sure that the crowds would obscure the panorama, and headed for Bar Harbor out of curiosity. Franklin Roosevelt had visited Bar Harbor often. As a young man, he would often send word to his mother at Campobello, 75 miles further east, to say that he was fog-bound, perhaps when there was no fog. Then he would sail into Bar Harbor to see friends and attend social gatherings.

I had heard the name quoted as an example of how the local dialect sounds: "Bah Habah" or "Baaba". Not surprisingly, the town was crowded with tourists and parking was impossible. I drove right through and continued south along the coast, hoping to find a cove where I could look for the eider ducks my guidebook said lived there year-round. The brochure made much of the tidal flats that were exposed twice a day, full of interesting things, but none were accessible through the private yards that cut off visitors like myself from the ocean. What's the point in mentioning them?

When I got frustrated with my cove quest, I turned off the narrow road following a sign to the Wild Gardens of Acadia. At least there would be a parking lot where I could plan my next move. The Wild Gardens were next to a Nature Center, which was closed. The garden was created to display the vegetation in different ecosystems of the island. Worth exploring, I thought. I stepped under the arch at the entrance and onto a shady path and paused to look around. In the silence, I heard a tiny crunching of leaves near my feet. I peered into the light-colored ground cover saw a bright black eye. Very near the eye was a long beak. I stared. I could detect no movement, but from the brown leaves only four feet in front of me the shape of a well-camouflaged bird materialized, the size of a robin but much pudgier and with a very long bill. My heart leaped. I chanted my bird watching instructions. Note everything you can before the bird flies. Don't rush to a book. The bird won't be there when you look again.

The bird had unusual bars across its crown, side to side, surely something to remember. I stared until I had it memorized, and still it did not move. Was it real? I carefully stepped backward so I wouldn't scare it and returned to Turtle, hoping the bird would be there when I returned. Leafing through my bird book, I checked the picture of a woodcock, a bird I had on my wish-to-see list. They are eastern game birds, and usually only seen as a blur when flushed by hunting dogs. I found the description. It looked like my bird. When I crept back to where I had seen the bird, it was still there. It matched my picture of an American woodcock perfectly. Plump, long bill, large head, secretive. Hooray for me. Another first sighting.

In disbelief, I wondered why that bird was just sitting there, not afraid of me. Was it tame? Were its wings clipped? I couldn't believe this bird was alive and remained motionless for me to study. No staff people were around to ask these important questions. I knew that birds that rely on camouflage will stay put, believing they are not seen. I think I made eye contact, and we watched each other. What a treasure.

October 3, New Hampshire

The next day, I pointed Turtle north and west. The weather was crisp and sunny, and I was eager to see the famous autumn leaves, spot any birds that happened in my path and find my moose, a wild one this time.

I followed Highway 113 across Maine, and then to Fryeburg in northern New Hampshire. Then I turned drove up an ancient valley full of hardwoods that had finally turned the promised brilliant colors. The rocky ridges of the Presidential Range, a popular winter skiing area, frame the valley. The road I drove is a scenic highway, but as I made my way through North Conway, I came upon the Factory Outlet Center, which was packed with cars and tour buses. How could those people turn their backs on the gorgeous day to shop? I stopped to see what I was missing, just in case, but after checking out the LL Bean store and a few others, I settled for an ice cream cone at Fanny Farmer's and moved on.

The Appalachian Trail intrigued me because I had hiked portions of the Pacific Crest Trail, the corresponding cross-country trail that passes through Oregon from Mexico to Canada. The Appalachian Trail is more heavily traveled, and every year thousands of people hike a portion or all of the 2,167 mile trail that stretches from Springer Mountain in north Georgia to Katahdin in Maine. Thru-hikers start in Georgia and follow the snowmelt north in order to be able to complete the hike in one year.

At Pinkham's Notch, I pulled into the parking lot next to a large building, which is a rest stop for hikers in the summer and a ski lodge in the winter. Across the street was a trailhead I couldn't pass up. Breathing in the heavenly day, I hiked straight up, following the sign toward Square Ledge. Hiking took a lot of attention on that trail. Roots distracted me from the walls of rock that hung over the path at just the height to give an inattentive hiker a good smack on the head. If the Appalachian Trail is like that, count me out. In any case, long haul hiking is not on my agenda.

In only half an hour I emerged from the trees onto the ledge. The colors. The Colors! The whole valley was a pallet of natural hues. Waves of ochre washed onto beaches of magenta, lime green swirled around forest green, yellow-orange-red, bright, somber, flashy and subtle hues blanketed the U-shaped valley from rim to rim. I shared the ledge with a family group that apparently took this particular hike every year at the peak leaf viewing time. They were respectful of the view and I envied them their experience. Moments like that need to be shared and we shared the silence.

I returned to the well-equipped lodge and showered. Hikers can stop here for a day or two and recover from their trek with showers, hot food in a restaurant, sleep in a bed and replace equipment. There were sturdy places to hang out; but no open flames, please, in the area that looked like the day room for skiers, or the dry room for wet transients.

Upstairs were hikers of all sorts. In the store, several older people with walking staffs, wool sweaters, well-preserved boots and varicose veins were poking among the guidebooks. They were obviously life long hikers and not about to quit. They had twenty or thirty years on me at least and were such an inspiration.

Resting on the stone steps outside, a group of young people sat draped over their enormous packs. Ah, youth. They looked sturdy enough to have been hiking all summer and I wondered if they were thru-hikers. One sign said that every year, 2,500 people attempt to hike the entire distance from Georgia to Maine. Hardy souls.

I felt a bit defensive at my lack of enthusiasm for this

challenging hike, but consoled myself with thoughts of other grueling physical challenges I have done: Mt. Kilimanjaro with the 80 women of Loitokitok Outward Bound School, where I climbed the day we reached the peak with a roaring headache due to the 19,000 foot altitude; sailing a 25 foot light fiberglass boat with my husband from Mazatlan to San Diego in November against strong winds, 30 days of soggy misery and anxiety; pedaling from Portland, Oregon to Los Mochis, Mexico before the convenient bike panniers for equipment were available. Now I prefer not to carry all my equipment on my back so my challenges are less physical.

My guidebook said that if there were moose to be seen, they would found in northern New Hampshire and Vermont, so I kept driving north. There were no signs telling me I couldn't stay at Pontook Reservoir, south of Errol, New Hampshire, so I did. I parked at the water's edge of a large parking lot. A line of trees surrounded the reservoir, cupped by a rim of hills. To my left, three pickups sat next to an informal boat ramp that parted the willows. Duck hunters, probably. It was unfortunate that I was hunting for birds to see during the hunting season. I can't time everything right. As it got dark, two guys returned in a skiff and canoe, and loaded them in two of the pick-ups along with dogs and canvas bags with duck-sized lumps in them, and drove off. Maybe the lumps were just their decoys, though limp mallards would have been fine with me. Lots of those.

Dinner was rehydrated creamed corn soup with tiny tatties sliced very thin into it. And two ginger cookies. I studied my maps for the most likely moose habitat. I was in no hurry. There was lots to see and many moose possible.

The last hunter packed up after dark, and I was alone with three orange utility trucks and a fully loaded log truck parked far to my right across the big lot. I did some yoga and was ready for bed. Then I discovered it was only 7:30 p.m. My sensors hadn't yet adjusted to the shortening days. The air temperature was very mild, in the seventies inside Turtle, and only down to the high forties at night, much warmer than Nova Scotia.

I planned to continue my moose hunt by rising before dawn to take a careful drive along the moose-infested roads. A wildlife brochure warned that a thousand pounds of moose in the road is trouble. A car's hood will slip under its belly, leaving the moose to smash through your windshield, that is, if you're bombing down the road not expecting, or wanting, to meet one. Since I would be on the alert, I didn't think it would be a problem.

The sky was beginning to lighten at 5:30 a.m. Only a few cars were on the road. Within sight of the lot, I passed a man walking toward the reservoir in camouflage, carrying a gun. Was I ignoring the obvious? It *was* duck hunting season and I wondered if it could also be moose season. If so, any smart ones were probably far away. Well, maybe a stupid moose was hanging around for me to see. I had seen a nice white tail buck the previous year in southeastern Oregon while deer hunters surrounded me, so maybe my luck would hold.

I drove the 13-mile scenic road along the Androscroggin River, where moose supposedly abound. Dawn broke, but the heavy fog muted the sun. Maybe my moose was out there at the edge of a clearing but I couldn't see him.

When Turtle was warm, I stopped for breakfast in one of the pullouts for tourists and fishermen. There was a marsh in front of me, so I hoped when it got light, I would see the body of my moose standing there like the one Julia saw in Maine.

Nope. No moose.

After breakfast, I walked around the area in case my moose was down the dusty road that led off into the woods.

Not even tracks.

I tidied up and pushed on. The water next to the road moved so slowly I thought it might be a lake, but the map showed the river. Then I passed another sign. "Moose crossing next 8 miles." Promises, promises.

At the Dixville Notch Wildlife Viewing Area I hiked from the parking area down a short path into the brush. It led to a covered viewing platform overlooking . . . the road. What an odd place for a viewing platform, I thought, but the information signs said the moose like to lick the road salt in the spring. But there were no moose that day. All that tasty salt had been licked away months ago.

Back in Turtle, I was studying my maps, when a pickup pulled up along side of me and a guy and his dog hopped out. He respectfully approached and shyly knocked on my side window. He was tall but looked harmless. I had to make that assessment rapidly. I know. Serial killers all look nice, too.

"How do you like your rig?" he said.

"Great. She's perfect for me." A rather lame opening, I thought. I offered to let him see inside, and he poked his head in, looked around, and withdrew to stand outside while I sat down on the step.

"Well, I want to know what you like and what you don't like because I just bought myself a 17-foot shell I want to make into something like that so I have something to sleep in when I'm out photographing. I'm tired of sleeping in motels far from the shoot and having to get up too early to get the good light."

He had no trouble knowing my gender, which was refreshing. It came out, delicately, when we discussed biffies.

"I suppose the built-in toilet works well for you. I think I'll go with a porta-potty since I won't need to use it as often," he said.

OK. Sometimes I do succumb to penis envy.

As we talked, the clouds moved in, the wind picked up a little and the temperature dropped noticeably.

"I'm looking for a moose. Have you seen any?" I asked.

"Oh, yes. I sure did. Scared the bejeezuz out of me. He was in a bog not far from here. He was a bull with huge horns. I jumped out of the car to take his picture and he walked right out of the bog, up onto the road and headed right for me! I didn't think he was going to stop. I'm not certain what the picture looks like. I jumped in the car so fast, I didn't care."

Aha. Maybe the moose experience should be shared with Turtle. Actually, inside Turtle. He gave me directions to his bog and wished me luck.

I chased around all afternoon, following one person's clue after another, without luck. As I drove slowly down the remote roads, peering into marshes, bogs and fields, hunters in their gun-bristling pickups would drive by me to get a good look. I think they were checking out their competition. After seeing I was no threat, they sped past me. Perhaps that's why there were no moose for me. I gave up.

Naïve as I was, it may be that my good fortune lay in not finding the moose. Had I known that a bull moose can weigh as much as 1400 pounds and stand up to 7 ½ feet at its shoulder with its heavy antlers reaching over 10 feet off the ground, I might not have been so eager to get a close view.

Got my afternoon Pepsi in a General Store in West Danville, Vermont back on Highway 2. The dark and creaky floor and the wall of post office boxes with metal doors, tiny windows and little dials reminded me of the Selma General Store in southern Oregon near my grandmother's ranch. During our summer visits, when I was little, my family shopped and picked up our mail there. We never had a box because we were not residents, but I watched with envy when someone else dialed their secret combination and pulled the folded envelopes out of the tiny boxes.

My mother chatted with Mrs. Burr while she packed our groceries in a cardboard box, grabbing the thin string from overhead and deftly wrapping it around the upturned flaps to enlarge the box. A quickly tied knot and break the string and we were ready to go. While my mother paid, I studied the shelf of penny candy behind the cash register, carefully deciding on my treat, adding up the prices to match the coins I held in my hand. Now, those same penny candies are a nickel at least.

The Vermont store had basic items along with the local crafts: hand sewn dolls, carvings, and sachets. I was poking around the display of canned goods when another female tourist in faux country clothes asked the proprietor, a middle aged woman who was sorting some papers behind the counter: "What's this about Take Back Vermont on the bumper stickers I see around?"

I'd wondered the same thing but hadn't thought to ask.

The proprietor said curtly, "Civil union."

"Oh?" the woman said, a little perplexed. I had read in a local paper that Vermont had a controversial ballot measure that would allow gays and lesbians to be legally joined in a civil union, and be eligible for the legal privileges of heterosexual married couples.

"Yes. They say it's a move backward," said the proprietor with a smirk, "Just like they said when they freed the slaves and gave women the vote."

"Oh, I see," said the visitor. The proprietor glanced in my direction. I smiled back and raised my eyebrows and my thumb.

The strong wind blew all the birds on Lake Champlain into hiding but the shale beach at the campground was made of fascinating rocks. I tried to skip some of the flat stones I found but on the first bounce the wind flipped them over and ruined the throw. Further along the beach, masses of flakes stood on edge like the carefully prepared patio of a formal Chinese garden. I'd seen the flaky shale, but never the more compressed blocky stones in another section. They looked like simple wooden kids toys, just an outline sanded smooth. I tucked a couple of the boxy rocks under my passenger seat for another souvenir.

The shower at Grand Island State Park charged 25 cents for five minutes of hot water, plenty for me, but it allowed the deposit of up to fifteen quarters! That's an hour and fifteen minutes for one shower. I was astonished, but I thought about it. I'd taken my fifteen-year-old niece on a trip and waited each morning while she indulged in a shower that lasted at least an hour, I'm sure. She would have stuffed that coin box full and been right at home in that shower.

October 5, Vermont

In the morning, fog draped the fields and forests when I finally found the office for the Missisquoi National Refuge in northern Vermont. There was no visitor's center, just a map to the nature trail, and a nice opportunity for a walk on a misty morning. I pulled on my waterproof boots and strode through the field behind the manager's office, up over a railroad berm and down into the shrubby natural area. Not far along the path, grooved chips like smiles of wood were scattered around the base of a hardwood tree at the edge of the creek. The fresh beaver gnaws that girdled the trunk would kill it soon. I pocketed one of the chips for my collection. Yesterday, that chip was a part of a living tree and now it was a souvenir.

As I stood, I caught a glimpse of ripples in the water, which I would like to think was the beaver, but I saw no more. Further down the trail, I poked my head through the brush and studied the creek. In a shadow, next to the far shore a duck paddled serenely, and its glossy emerald plumage and sleek drooping crest blazed through the gloom. My feet danced inside my boots at the find, but my first wood duck startled and flew when it spotted me. I had to work on stealth, or I wouldn't be able to study these birds.

Breakfast was at Swanton's own Country Kitchen Café, Swanton, Vermont. The cheese in the omelet reminded me of that awful stuff you get on airplanes that comes in little aluminum wrappers with a cow on the front and never spoils, but that isn't a problem because the packets are impossible to open. The cafe was the kind I like anyway. It was old but clean, with the standard breakfast menu inside a sticky plastic cover: eggs, bakery items, hash browns, toast, juice.

A salesman in his mid-thirties stood in the doorway to the kitchen, which was right next to my table. He was trying to persuade the owner, a woman about his age who leaned against the other side of the doorframe, to install his brand of commercial coffee maker. She was happy with the one she had, thank you, so they chatted for a while. The Country Kitchen Cafe is the choice of the town regulars. She's on by herself when they arrive about six or six thirty, and they are there to drink her coffee and gossip until about eight. If that's all they buy, it's a wonder she stays in business, but maybe they bring the family in for dinners. Maybe they tip well. Or maybe that socializing is what binds their community together and is more important than the quality of the coffee or the size of the tip.

He managed to take the conversation back to his coffee maker several times, and she said "No" every time, at first politely with an oblique comment, and then a little more clearly.

"Look," he said after the third or fourth time, "Don't make up your mind right now. You think about it, and I'll come back next week and see what you think." I felt like standing up and asking him if he was deaf, but she didn't seem to need my help. I admired his tenacity, however, and wished I'd had a bit of it when I had tried to raise money for various causes.

Vermont does not allow billboards. In urban Burlington, road signs for upcoming shops or attractions are limited to tiny strips of information painted on a four-inch by three-foot pieces of wood nailed to a post with up to three others on the same post. I loved the lack of clutter until I wanted to actually find out what was ahead of me as I drove. There's enough room on each sign for two lines per attraction. The lettering on the first line was readable two car lengths away, but the second line with directions was smaller. The more that had to be said, the smaller the print. "Bill's General Store, third right, two blocks on your left." "Mama Jane's Crafts and Books, local crafts, dolls, wind chimes, 1/4 mile." I had to read all of them while watching four lanes of cars, construction barriers and lights, simultaneously deciding which sign to pay attention to while absorbing the information at 45 miles an hour. Slowing down was not an option because I was being pushed along by SUVs who knew where they were headed and wished I'd quit sightseeing. Once I passed a sign, that was it, no reiteration further along. If there was something that interested me, and I was able to catch the directions, I still needed help. What is a "right" among big roads, small roads and road-sized driveways? For respite, I turned into the large parking lot for Shelburne Museum, south of Burlington on Highway 7. My brain was overloaded.

I asked a couple just leaving the exhibit if it was worth the time, and they said it was good, but they lacked that gushing enthusiasm I wanted before committing myself to a hefty entrance fee. In the preview barn, I saw videos and teasers for the place. It seemed huge, with 39 galleries of art, Americana, architecture, and was way more than I could absorb that day after struggling with the directional signs. I like to approach museums with a fresh mind so I can take in as much as possible. And at $17.50 to enter, I'd really have to want to stay, which I didn't.

A quiet walking trail is what I really wanted after driving a while, but they aren't always where I need them.

As I continued south toward Addison I pondered my lack of interest in that museum. When I was traveling across Nebraska the previous year, I was driving through open and unpopulated areas. Uncluttered. Lacking stimuli. Boring. My brain was crying for new input. A museum was a welcome break. On my way to Alliance, Nebraska I saw the sign to the Museum of Fur Trade, east of Chadron. The nondescript flat building contained a tiny space with amazing artifacts all about the fur trade, not only in the area but also worldwide. Maps, traps, furs, stuffed animals and skeletons, old boots and guns. It was a real find.

Also near Alliance, Car Henge had been on my "to see" list since I saw an article about it years ago. It's a replica of Stone Henge made of old cars painted gray and planted in a field. Now that was a work of interest. Tongue in cheek art. One other car stopped while I was there. I loved it, though the townspeople didn't when it was first created. I'm not sure they do now. I thought I'd find at least post cards for sale in the town, but didn't find one and no one seemed interested when I asked. I wondered if they appreciated that the treasure at the edge of town could bring tourist cash, if they would see it as something of value.

My other favorite museum was Harold Warp's Pioneer Village in Minden, Nebraska, See How America Grew. After miles and days of relatively unchanging and unpopulated driving, I was ready for some stimulation, and I wasn't disappointed. On twenty acres, 28 buildings and the grounds were filled with mechanical items like cars, washing machines, phonographs, tractors, and locomotives. Every model made until about 1950. One building had a series of complete kitchens up to the 1950's, one for each decade. Huge collections of guns, money, thimbles, firefighting equipment, sugar bowls filled the buildings. There were old cabins, merry-go-rounds, jails, post offices, a sod house, a tiny church; all of which had been moved from their original spots. It would be a wonderful place for a writer to do background research.

An article in one of the newspapers I picked up mentioned that Dead Creek Wildlife Refuge, outside of Addison, Vermont was welcoming the annual flock of snow geese with celebrations and tours on the coming weekend. Certainly worth investigating. When I arrived about 3 o'clock, a handful of expectant people dressed against the chilly wind were waited on the viewing platform but there were no geese in sight.

I joshed with one birder who was stomping around the parking area to keep warm. I'd passed a few geese down the road, and said glibly, "Maybe someone forgot to tell the geese they were supposed to meet here." Ha ha. He smiled but didn't comment. I am embarrassed to admit my arrogance, and had I asked a few questions, I might have saved myself a fruitless hunt. I decided to keep moving, hoping to run across the flock in another field, which I didn't. When I returned to the viewing area less than two hours later, it was full of geese, still settling in. Apparently the show was over because the last birder was just leaving. I'd missed most of the fly in. Drat.

A thousand gabbling snow geese, with a few Canada geese mixed in, were settling on a slightly elevated plot of land across a field in front of the viewing platform. Lines of the white geese with black wingtips still flew in from the north. They landed among the geese who had arrived earlier, exploding a whole group into a chattering white cloud. The flock glided to another spot and landed again. Even though I had missed the massive fly-in, what I did see was exciting and I hoped I'd be more patient if another opportunity to see them presented itself.

Life goes on around those birds. The area is managed for the geese, but cows graze in nearby fields. While I watched, a farmer rounded up his herd of Holsteins and pointed them back to a distant barn for their afternoon milking. They strung out in a long line between the geese and me, sauntering at a cow's unhurried pace. The mature cows perked their ears at the noisy birds and huffed. The calves eyed the geese, kicked up their heels and threw their heads as they lumped and rocked to the front of the line.

Two fields away, another farmer harvested corn with a loud machine. A truck full of grain lumbered slowly over the muddy road, past the geese, and onto the paved road. The geese didn't seem to notice.

On my fruitless side trip while the birders waited, I had driven down Highway 17 to hunt for the missing geese. I didn't want to get completely lost, so I looked for the DAR State Park as a checkpoint. It was clearly marked on the map. Way past where the DAR S.P. should have been, I stopped at Chimney Point Historical Site to try and figure out where I was.

The previous day, I found another state park down a long mud road, which was closed. The large parking lot was the giveaway, however. I had parked at the barred gate and walked in to select bright blood red and lemon yellow leaves for my collection. However, I noticed there were no signs indicating what this was. They take down ALL the signs. No "Here we are but we're sorry we're closed." Rather, "We don't exist any more. Go away." Never mind that a stranger to the area might need to know its location for navigational purposes.

DAR State Park may exist on a map but unless you know that all Vermont state parks have old dark brown buildings with white trim at the entrance, and two posts holding up a frame with a pair of limp chains hanging from the top, you're out of luck. I discovered the missing park right where it was supposed to be on my return trip, limp chains and all.

The information system for Vermont is nuts. I needed at least four different publications to figure out where to go that evening, and even that number wasn't enough. One brochure told me where to see wildlife, but nothing about what kind to expect: birds? Moose? Are they seasonal? What? And no directions. Just a spot on a roadless map. Sometimes a clue such as "Route 13." Another brochure listed state parks but I had to use yet another to get the information on when they close for the season and what's there to do and see. Which campgrounds are near the wildlife? Another brochure. Kind of like a puzzle, and me without a big table to spread them all out.

At Branburg State Park, south of Middlebury, Vermont, I spent a drizzly night at the edge of a meadow rimmed with trees. Numbered posts around the perimeter indicated the campsites, which had tables but no electricity.

It was supposed to rain off and on through the weekend, after which all the campgrounds would close. The people in the site next to me were determined to camp this last weekend of the season. A huge blue tarp covered their family-sized tent. A Penske rental truck half full of boxes and piles of tarps was backed up the their site, and the tables were loaded with food, lanterns pots and cutlery, as if the sun were out. They wore full rain suits and I never got a good look at any of them. They were just yellow ghosts that drifted in and out of the tent and trucks or stood staring at the flames of a nice fire. I admired their tenacity. Inside Turtle I was warm and dry, and felt even cozier as I remembered wet camps I'd experienced when caught during backpacking trips in bad weather. The patter of the raindrops on the roof made me feel nesty, so after a bowl of hot soup, I climbed into my warm bed to read and doze.

Residual engine heat keeps Turtle warm in the evenings but after a cool night, she's chilly inside. The next morning, I donned my fleece pants and jacket to keep warm for breakfast and stared out into a dark day. The drizzle had almost stopped for a while, so I took an invigorating hike up an old dirt road nearby. After a shower, we set out to climb over the Green Mountains. Turtle was roasty toasty again after a bit of driving but the day was heavy with the threat of more rain. The low fog on the hillsides was so thick, it didn't matter how red the foliage was. I couldn't see it or the mountains, which were hardly worthy of the title by western measures. It's all relative. "The Appalachian Hills" doesn't quite have the same majestic ring as "The Appalachian Mountains".

I turned onto Highway 100 and needed a map check. Magically, a charming little cafe appeared, all by itself with a couple of cars with Vermont plates parked next to it. A local eatery. I anticipated some good gossip, but eavesdropping wasn't very fruitful. The lunch crowd had yet to appear, only a few seats were taken and the occupants seemed content to chew in peace. Those Vermonters were as terse in reality as in reputation.

I had a hot bowl of ho'made turkey soup and the special of the day, "Mac 'n' Cheese". The special for the following day was Shepherd's pie and I almost stayed over to try some. I hadn't had Shepherd's pie in since my mother made it for me when I was a kid. But, there was still a lot of day left, so I moved on.

The new road was busier, and I had to speed up or be run over by trucks. I hate that. It was drizzling again, but I was warm and smug because I'd had my exercise hiking and a hot meal. I headed for Rhode Island at a mosey.

By the next break, in a pull-off near Lake Rescue, the rain had stopped. The lake was so calm that the reflection of every leaf was crisp and clear. In the muted light, the leaf show was subtler than the previous days I could enjoy the nuances in the interplay of colors. Oranges prevailed. Occasional flames of red or bursts of yellow punctuated the predominant tones of green and brown.

To stop and admire the leaves on that narrow two-lane road was a death-defying act. Many signs said "NO parking on active road," but no one seemed to notice. I passed several cars precariously parked, barely off the pavement, the driver pointing his camera at the trees, and the endless traffic passing dangerously in both directions.

All over Vermont, I'd been seeing signs that read "Redemption Center" and I thought the Christians had really gotten aggressive, maybe in response to the civil union campaign. Signs that jutted right out to the edge of the road seemed brassy, all right. Some were painted high on buildings or on barrels next to a church. Others were painted on a sandwich board outside some large, unoccupied building. It was fundamentalist recruitment to an extent I had never seen.

To my relief, I discovered the truth when I passed a lot where the redemption process was actually occurring. A woman took two lumpy paper bags out of the trunk of her car and gave them to a kid, who pulled out the empty cans and bottles and tossed them in a bin. He called a number to another man who made out a receipt and gave her some money. A center to redeem your cans and bottles. Redemption for plastic and metal, not people. Whew.

Rhode Island does not have many public camping areas so I spent the night at a private camping enclave where people own their site, park a camper or trailer and visit every weekend. The bulletin board in the office was full of notices to people on how to prepare for winter. This was the last weekend of the season. Tanks had to be dumped and vehicles wrapped for winter or moved to another location. In the morning, the tasks were proceeding at a leisurely pace while kids rode their bike and people stopped to chat along the road.

October 7, Rhode Island

Cape Cod was my destination for the night because my Elderhostel session started the next day in Provincetown. The morning was sunny and warm when I sidled across Rhode Island to cross the scenic Narragansett Bay on a high bridge. Once across the bay, I took the exit to Newport and was suddenly sucked into a stream of traffic that spit me out at the visitor's center along with half the population of the eastern seaboard. There was a Disneyland quality to the buses and the masses of people that challenged the tiny access streets and gaped at the quaint buildings.

The restrooms in the visitor's center were unable to cope with buses loaded mostly with women. Lines snaked out the door and across the lobby the whole time I was there. I loved having Turtle and especially her biffy in places like that.

Tickets for the popular tours to the big mansions were sold out for that day. After the Civil War, wealthy industrialists began to buy Newport shoreline property for summer homes. During the Gilded Age from 1890 to 1914, Newport was another summer retreat for upper class social life like Bar Harbor and Campobello. The ballroom of the John Jacob Astor's could only hold 400 people, so when they threw a ball, they had to choose 400 people from off the social register. From the limitations of that ballroom arose the coveted identification of "The 400" who counted in New York society. Blame the architect. The wealthy who summered in Newport never mixed with the townspeople, who thought the houses were too grandiose and who were never invited to them anyway.

I picked up a map for a bike tour around the famous Ten Mile Drive that skirted the curving shore among the mansions. I unloaded my bike, which needed cosmetic care after miles of dirt and days of rain. Helmets seemed to be optional, but I was glad for mine as the cars full of gawkers weaved by me on the narrow streets. Bicycling on cobblestones isn't pleasant, but soon I left the center of town and biked on asphalt around a point where huge houses sat on mini-farm sized lots. Signs warned to be careful where you stop or you are trespassing, especially near the beaches. Not open to the public. How unfriendly. Occasionally, I could linger and enjoy the view of the bay in a tiny park or at the entrance to someone's driveway, but most of the waterfront was obscured by private houses behind tall hedges. What a contrast to the open beaches of Nova Scotia.

The streets on the bike loop were wide and each mansion was the size of a resort hotel. I tried not to be judgmental, but really, how many rooms does one family need? Were they edifices of physical distraction to compensate for lack of personal feelings of adequate power, I wondered? How some things stay the same. But I was there only to observe and I pedaled on.

Toward the end of the tour loop, signs in front of many of the opulent mansions proclaimed they were open for tours, for a fee, of course. People with the coveted tickets entered for the tour. I pedaled up the long driveways and by the time I could see the signs that said I wasn't welcome without a ticket, I'd seen all I wanted.

I chained my bike outside "Rosecliff," designed by Stanford White for Nevada silver heiress, "Tessie" Fair Oelrichs in 1902. The imposing U-shaped columned house with extensive gardens is supposed to have been modeled on the Grand Trianon, the garden retreat of French Kings at Versailles. Its hostess welcomed the wealthy to spectacular parties at the peak of the Gilded Age.

More recently, the mansion was the setting for several movies, including The Great Gatsby and True Lies.

Without a ticket, I was unable to see inside the houses, and from the pictures in the brochure, taking a walk on the sea wall, the walkway that wrapped its way along many of the properties, was probably the healthier pursuit. The walkway was built so the fishermen could get to their boats after the tycoons bought up their modest seaside fisherman's houses and property. How kind.

The class distinctions in the east are a surprise to me. In the Portland, where a prominent family has only had three or four generations in the area to establish themselves, there seems to be less distance between people with wealth and those without. Here in the East, many families are proud of their Mayflower roots, and the separation between them and newer arrivals has had more time to solidify. The physical manifestations seem more ensconced in the culture of the place. We certainly have big houses, but they do not have the history of generations that make them repositories of cultural significance and the basis for the elite behaviors that make me uncomfortable.

The irony is that I have distinguished roots myself. The Pilgrims decided to immigrate to the New World in order to practice their form of religion that was not supported in England. They had tried living in Holland, but missed all things English. By moving the colony to the New World, they could maintain their English habits and their chosen religious practices.

The organizers were practical men. The trip would be expensive, so they negotiated with some merchants to underwrite the trip in return for their cooperation in building commerce with the New World. One third of the passengers on the Mayflower were Pilgrims and the rest were merchant adventurers. Several later ships with the same mix of merchants and Pilgrims followed the Mayflower.

One of the merchants that made the trip possible was Thomas Tilden, who came over on the "Anne" in 1623 and was allotted three shares of land in what is now Scituate, MA, about 18 miles north of Plymouth. In 1632, his brother, Nathaniel Tilden, my direct ancestor through the Odell line, followed on the "Hercules" to settle in the same area, possibly on one of the shares allotted to Thomas.

I've been waiting for some person with the gall to wave their Mayflower forbearers around, ready to drop into the conversation that one of my ancestors helped finance the first Mayflower voyage, let the Pilgrims get established in the New World and came over later, which seemed the wiser thing to do but the subject doesn't come up very often among my friends.

On a sunny fall day, the seawall walk was fabulous, and I loved the diversity of the other walkers: old, young, people of all ethnicities, some speaking unfamiliar languages. I did recognize Japanese, Spanish and French, and there were some Balkan and Scandinavian words that drifted by me as I rubbed shoulders with the other people out enjoying the glorious day.

After my walk, I found the town library, picked up my emails, typed out a few replies and peddled back to Turtle.

Back on the road to Cape Cod, I took only a few wrong turns trying to get out of Newport and finally made it onto the Cape Cod hook. After driving on the limited access highway for a while, I needed to check my map for the directions to Maurice's RV Park, my night's destination halfway down the hook. There was no place to pull over for miles, so I turned down one of the few roads, past a sign that said "Fort Hill." It looked like a public place and I assumed there would be a parking lot.

Right off the highway, I found myself on a narrow street fully shaded by trees. There was a viewpoint ahead, according to the next sign, so I figured I could turn around there. A sign at a tiny intersection said "No vehicles over 20'" which indicated some cramping at the viewpoint. Turtle is only seventeen feet long, so I continued, ever hopeful. Where the tunnel of trees ended, the road opened onto the small parking lot a few hundred yards before the actual viewpoint. It was already full of expensive cars, and people in formal dress were streaming down the road away from me toward the viewpoint. I was crashing a wedding reception. I couldn't turn around, so I kept going until I could see there were only more cars and lots more people ahead of me. In desperation, I stopped and signaled the car behind me to stop so I could get turned around in what space there was. With much to-ing and fro-ing and smiling lamely at the drivers behind me, I was able to use the narrow grass verge that edged the road to turn around and GOT OUT of there.

At Maurice's RV Park, where I finally was able to settle for the night, I gave Turtle a nice bath, and tidied up for my week's stay in Provincetown. I wasn't due at the Elderhostel program until the next afternoon, so I had the morning to explore Cape Cod.

On the map, I spotted Great Island, which was a peninsula near Wellfleet. My mind flooded with memories of the trip I took to Great Island with my family when I was in high school. The images were crisp and foggy, as memories are. I remember peering out of the back window as my father drove us among rolling sand dunes planted with a few huge Victorian cottages. He pointed out the houses and told us who lived in them when he and his family were summer guests of the Chaces, who owned Great Island. My father was delighted to discover that one of his childhood friends, Clover, still lived there. He and I visited Clover the next day and I remember clearly sitting in her large and warm Victorian kitchen. She was pleased to steam some clams for my father, something he had not enjoyed since those years. I don't think my mother liked them and I'd never eaten steamed clams. My father and Clover reminisced on youthful adventures with friends and relatives among the dunes and on the beaches. I twisted to look out the big kitchen window to see the grassy dunes, the scene of their escapades. Ghosts from the past drifted past me, gangs of sun-brown kids with picnic baskets and beach pails, laughing and calling to each other. My father devoured his share of the clams and paid no attention to the fact that I was just sucking the butter off the soft bodies.

The tone my father used when he described how his family

came to be on Great Island was that of a poor relative. They came at the pleasure of his father's wealthy friend, Malcolm Chace, who knew from Brown University. He even said, "He felt sorry for Dad." My grandfather had never seemed poor to me. He owned a nice Victorian house in Kansas City, anyway. Still, for one man to own a whole peninsula and several large houses was a lot for one man.

What I could not remember was how we got to Great Island. The map shows a peninsula named Great Island stretching south and into the bay formed by the Cape Cod hook and it was a national park. I couldn't imagine that the stretch of dunes and houses I had seen becoming a park.

The next morning, I drove through Wellfleet and out the Chequessett Neck Road, following the signs to Great Island, a part of the Cape Cod National Seashore. There were no houses perched on dunes, only narrow driveways that headed away from the shore into dense brush. My first stop was at a remote beach access with a small parking area. I stopped in front of the informational sign, blocking the only car in the lot, and considered whether to get out and hike or to go back to the larger, more developed area. I decided to stay and carefully backed around the other car. I watched out my left mirror, moving dead slow, but as I eased into my spot, I glanced into my right mirror to see the startled face of a woman who was climbing out of the passenger side of a car parked less than three feet from Turtle. Where did she come from? The car must have whipped in behind me just as I decided to back up. After that too-close encounter, I was too rattled to stay.

Driving back to the main parking lot I kept asking myself, where are the houses? Where is any evidence of the Chaces? Of Clover, of my visit in 1958? Did I imagine it all?

At the trailhead to the bay beach, I studied the trail map. A youngish couple emerged from the patch of pine trees that obscured the beach. We fell into hikers' conversation until, finally,

I said, "I visited this area with my family about 1958 and I remember big houses on sandy dunes. Do you have any idea where they might be? I know we were on Great Island."

She thought a moment and said, "My family has lived here for years and I know this became a National Park about 1960, but I don't recall any houses out here, ever."

Whoa. Twilight Zone. I KNOW we were on Great Island with my father. Large Victorian houses do not go unnoticed. Nor are they torn down without discussion she would have heard.

I could ponder the mystery while I hiked. Break Beach Hill sounded like an interesting destination that promised a good view. I waded through soft sand and out of the tunnel of pitch pines. Once on the flat, firm sand, damp from a recent rain, hiking was brisk and invigorating. A dune on my right prevented me from seeing the ocean. The expanse of sand on my left hid the shoreline with the bay but I could see the town of Wellfleet across the water. A gentle sea breeze blew off the harbor and at the call of gulls, I looked up to watch them glide serenely on the air. When I paused to soak in the sun breaking through the overcast, I looked back and saw a few houses peering over the dune near where I had just been. They looked relatively new and modern. I bet there was a fuss when they were built. But they were not Victorians, nor were they on the rolling, grass-covered dunes I remembered. At home, I had a picture of my father as a tot standing on one of those dunes to sharpen my memory. He is about two in the picture, wearing a straw hat with a black ribbon and light, knitted shorts over his bulky diapers. He is holding a shovel in one hand and a little pail in the other. If my aunt's recollections of him are accurate, he probably was caught that day leaving his family for an adventure of his own.

Could a difference in the season make a difference in the nature and appearance of the dunes?

At a neck of the peninsula, the path passed through a patch of trees and I spotted a marker in a grove of shore pines. Aha. A clue, maybe.

A quote from Governor William Bradley of the Mayflower was engraved on the bronze plaque telling me that the Mayflower first landed on that very spot. I looked around to imagine the scene. Sea-tired voyagers trod ashore in their high hats and shiny black shoes with big silver buckles on both and capes over their shoulders. Whoa. They probably weren't dressed in their finery, even though my kindergarten books pictured that scene. They had to be rather grubby after months at sea, and they were probably looking for fresh water and some game for food. It may not even have been their first landfall, as signs I saw later seemed to indicate.

The trees I could see could not have been sprouted when the travelers landed; the dunes may even have been arranged in a different pattern. No matter. This was the spot where they landed. But the land could not support a colony, and the settlers soon moved onto the mainland. One of Bradley's descendents, Priscilla Alden Bartlett (1939-1962), did live on that patch of land more recently and loved it. She married Alexander I. Henderson, but from the dates, it was not a long marriage. She was the one who donated the land to the public. No mention of the Chaces or of houses anywhere nearby. Another disappointment.

After my hike, I returned to Wellfleet and drove into more cramped streets. Happily, I found a large visitor's parking lot behind the old buildings. The Historical Museum was around the corner, in a small white house with black shutters, but it was closed for the season. A note taped to the door said to "Please call Myrtle" and a phone number underneath. I did not call Myrtle, thinking to do so later.

Only after returning home did I discover the answer to my dilemma in re-reading some of the notes from my father's sister. On a picture of her, my father and their two siblings she wrote cryptically, "Great Island, near Hyannis Port." I looked on my map. There is *another* peninsula labeled Great Island on the south side of the Cape Cod hook. That must have been where we visited. What a relief. My mind isn't going quite yet.

The directions to the motel where I was to meet my Elderhostel group suggested skirting Provincetown, but I wanted to see a little of it before settling in. It is the oldest continuous art colony, popular for over one hundred years and recently has been attracting gays and lesbians looking for a safe place to party.

I drove Turtle down street lined with tidy beach houses and a few quaint shops. The streets got progressively narrower as I approached the shore. Commercial Street was almost impassable. It was not really a street and not commercial but it was right next to the bay where the first commercial activity would have occurred. I thought I really was going to get stuck. Cars were parked on the shore side and a fence cramped the other with no space for even a sidewalk I could drive on in a pinch. Turtle isn't all that big, the length and breadth of a hefty pickup, but the people strolling down the street, who had to turn sideways to get past Turtle's rear view mirrors, looked at me and grimaced, like, who let her on this street? I wanted to roll down my window and yell that I didn't want to be there, either. The street signs didn't exactly tell me I was going to end up on a cattle path! But I refrained. The morning's near collision filled me with dread that I might have to back all the way out to the highway. Take me back to Montana. NOW. I was near panic when I was spit out of the cramped road onto a roundabout in front of my motel, which had, thankfully, a large parking lot.

I had planned to check in early and do some laundry. Certainly a place like Provincetown, hangout for famous writers, gay people and tourists, would have a laundromat. If I were lucky, the motel would have one, but I was wrong both times. I had to backtrack half an hour to Orleans/Brewster; a normal-looking town with fewer services aimed at tourists and some people who would admit their clothes needed a wash.

Laundry can't be rushed, but I was going to be late for the first dinner of my Elderhostel group, so I grabbed my damp clothes out of the dryer and hurried back to the motel, via the recommended route, avoiding those itty-bitty streets. I threw t-shirts, shorts, underwear and socks over all the furniture in my room and rushed down to dinner. Somewhere in the sea of faces was my roommate. I hoped to meet her in time to warn her of the explosion of clothing waiting in our room.

Early October on Cape Cod

The Elderhostel program was a nice break in my trip, four nights in a motel, but maybe I put a little too much store in the mention of birds in the course description; birds, beaches and marshes was the promise. The few birders among our group of forty found each other, and did some birding on our own but most of the course was about the marshes, shore and whales, which I usually find interesting, but having hoped for more birding, I was disappointed.

I did not shift from a freewheeling wanderer to a groupie with speed and grace. On one expedition, we were dropped off in the same parking lot where I had crashed the wedding party. We were there to learn about salt marshes, the coastal wetlands so rich in marine life. The one we studied was in a protected part of an estuary where spartina, a type of grass, dominates and provides shelter for young fish that eat the detritus that settles on the mud bottom. Salt marshes are critical habitat for many marine organisms in certain stages of growth. I thought of the many marshes near my home where I had watched birds, and understood their importance and the threat to their survival with increased appreciation.

During the marsh talk, we wandered at the edge of the grassy mud plain, but soon I got restless. I needed to walk faster than the stroll of the group and I wanted a little time for myself. The togetherness had begun to grate on me. The leader said we were close to our destination, so I went on ahead, down the trail into the woods. I knew where we began the walk, and at a fork, turned in that direction. After following a wooden ramp over the woodsy marsh for longer than I thought I should be walking, I began to worry. I walked faster, relieved when I finally spotted the parking lot through the thinning brush. But when I exited the cover, the bus was not there. From a corner of my memory, I dredged up snatches of a conversation I'd overheard in passing between our leader and the bus driver about moving the bus to meet us at another spot. No matter. A Park Ranger was standing by his vehicle in the little lot, so I asked him for a ride—not an unreasonable request, I thought.

Not a chance. Not his job. No suggestions, either.

So, I accosted a couple in their late sixties who were pulling out of the lot in a roomy sedan, and pleaded with them. At least it sounded like pleading to me. I don't often ask for help. The balding man in the driver's seat understood and told me to hop in. His gaunt wife was sympathetic, and turned around in her seat to ask about the program, which I described with most of my attention on finding the bus. I directed him down the road where I thought the bus might be. Luckily, I was right, and as the yellow monster lumbered toward us, my benefactor waved his hand out his window to stop it. I jumped out with a quick "Thanks" to the friendly couple and climbed aboard. Everyone on the bus was surprised at my appearance. I hadn't been missed. One of the women on staff wrinkled her brow as she asked me how I had gotten separated and had the grace to vow to count heads next time the group got off the bus. I resolved to tell someone when I decided to leave the group. It would have been a long walk to dinner.

The whaling trip on the fourth day proved to be a wonderful boat ride. We had waited for the stormy weather to abate, and were rewarded with the sight of about twenty whales during the four hour trip. Barnacle encrusted-backs slid across the surface of the water and fountains of misty air blew into the sky followed by hearty gasps for air. The whales seemed to be lazing along, surfacing to glimpse the tourists who were snapping their picture. Several whales breached before plunging into the depths, providing us with a view of a dramatic tail flip before they plunged into the depths. We saw mostly finback and humpback whales and felt lucky to see so many at the end of their migratory season.

As we pulled out of the slip, I spotted three common eider ducks swimming among the boats. They have a basic duck shape except for the very unusual sloping forehead, looking like someone with a pronounced Roman nose. The backs of the males are white and the sides are black.

I knew about eiders long before I was a birder. When I was backpacking in winter, before synthetic insulation, I wore a jacket filled with eider down to keep warm in the coldest weather. Duck down from farmed ducks was less resilient and the quills were stiffer making them more likely to poke through the nylon outer layer. Eider down also keeps its insulating qualities better than the other kinds when wet, an advantage in the rainy Northwest. A rush of remorse washed over me as I realized that the down had to have come from dead ducks. Fortunately, down has been replaced by synthetics in utility and popularity.

At sea, my birder friends and I saw several kinds of pelagic birds. Between the whale sightings, we spotted two varieties of shearwater, the Sooty and Greater. They are the size of gulls but with longer wings and large nostril tubes on their bills, an adaptation that most birds that remain at sea for long periods have for filtering seawater. The Sooty is charcoal colored while the Greater shearwater has a dark brown cap and white underbelly with a dark back.

By the end of that day I was growing eager to get back onto my own schedule. Nice as they all were, forty people were hard for me to be around all day.

I worried how I would get around New York City. Interstate 95 was the shortest route, but it ran right through the middle of the city and I hate to admit it, but besides the aggressive drivers I feared, I worried about having to get off the throughway for gas or an emergency and finding myself in an unfriendly neighborhood, vulnerable to the menacing behaviors I associate with gangs, poverty and densely packed, angry people. On a visit to New York, the driver of my taxi would not drive through Harlem even during the day, which left a lasting impression. Alone in Turtle, I feel visible and vulnerable in dangerous places and I do my best to avoid them.

At my last dinner, a couple who lived in the area shared their route around the northern perimeter of the New York City. It sounded good to me.

I skipped the last meeting and left early Friday morning hoping to avoid weekend traffic. Once off Cape Cod, I drove west until I crossed the Hudson River north of West Point, upriver from the city.

I was relieved to be out of New England, with its tiny roads and masses of people. Even the wild places were well worn with overuse. I left behind the anxiety of almost getting wedged into that tiny street in Provincetown and having to navigate endless spaghetti-looped roads that twisted and wandered as if they had forgotten where they were going.

When I turned south onto I-87, high berms covered with small trees flanked the road, giving the impression of a pastoral interlude before diving back into northern New Jersey sprawl. Toward the end of the day, I ran into weekend traffic outside of Philadelphia. What a surprise. I thought I was on the eastern shore, but New Jersey is a small state and soon I regained the Atlantic coast.

After dark, I backed into my spot at the Shady Pines Camping Resort, coming within inches of nailing my bicycle to a tree, to the entertainment of my neighbors. I caught glimpses of their curtains flicking as I settled into my site.

I entered in my log that I had covered more than 500 miles that day. The road to new adventures waited and New York City was behind me. I had space to breathe.

October 14, New Jersey

Thousands of yapping snow geese were tinted pink by the dawn glow at Brigantine/Forsythe Wildlife Refuge. The dingy gray backs of the juveniles, only weeks from their nests in the north, subdued the sparkle of the undulating mass, giving it depth and texture. Over the top of the salt marsh grasses and across a protected bay the sun glinted off the windows of Atlantic City, less than ten miles to the south. Turtle was parked half off the deserted road next to a pond surrounded by dikes and grasses. About two hundred of the small geese floated on the water, grumbling and chittering. It seemed to take lots of conversation for them to wake up. On the dikes, some of the birds hunkered down while others waddled aimlessly, warming up maybe. A chorus from more geese rose from the grasses. As the sun rose higher, flocks of a few hundred birds at a time lifted into the air in a thunder of flapping wings and splashing feet. Once airborne, they were like dry leaves in the wind, circling to get their bearings until one of them led the way north or south, still squawking. As I watched, I puzzled at the mystery of bird leadership. Is there a lead bird they follow? Who decides which way to go and when? Is all that noise part of a decision process? Does each individual stay with the same fellow travelers, or does it lift off only when a flock leaves at the time it is ready? What would that term, "ready," mean to a goose? To my disappointment, I learned later that those were questions biologists have yet to answer.

I saw the entire launch of the thousands of snow geese, start to finish like a real birder. I felt as if I'd passed a birding milestone, making up for my naiveté in Vermont.

After most of the birds had left, I tidied up and drove inland to check out another part of the refuge. Exiting a patch of trees, I passed a harvested grain field full of geese grazing on the leftovers. The Greater Snow Geese that winter in the area feed on the bulbs and roots of the marsh grasses, pulling them up and killing them entirely. In the 1970s and 80s the high numbers of geese depleted the available food and the population dropped dramatically. Conservationists began to plant corn and grains in nearby fields to take the pressure off the marsh plants. The plan has been successful and over the last 15 years, the well-nourished geese have been flourishing.

Another reason for the population growth is that their breeding grounds in southern Canada are warming, resulting in more successful broods, which then ravage the coastal breeding habitat. Their response is to move inland, threatening more areas. In the 1990s their population began to grow and now is predicted to double every ten years. Steps are being taken to curb their numbers, estimated at about 800,000. Hunting bag limits have been increased both in Canada and the U.S. Wildlife managers are draining the ponds where they roost at night and planting less of the corn and grains in order to force the geese out of the refuges and into hunting areas.

As I write this, a flash of anger rises. Anger that the swirling abundance of geese was not something I could relish unconditionally. Anger at the feeling that we humans have disrupted the natural cycles of so many species that their own regulatory mechanism, survival of the fittest, has been too skewed to ever work again. Must I always have to temper my appreciation of wildlife by acknowledging that there are too many of one species, too few of another? For example, starlings are gorgeous birds, with their green-black metallic feathers that flash in the sunlight, their crazy songs and joyful cacophony from the crown of a tree. Watching fearless house sparrows forage among outdoor diners always lifts my spirits, but both species are invaders, and drive out the natives. There are times when I wish I didn't know all this. Perhaps this discomfort is balanced by the glimpse of a rare species, as long as it is rare for reasons not related to human intervention so I don't feel responsible for the scarcity.

Leaving the snow geese behind, I continued south toward Cape May. The traffic was quite busy on the Garden State Parkway, and I created a new use for my "troll bell", made of two small bells and a horsehair tassel I bought at a rodeo in Oregon. It hangs on the wall over my left shoulder, where I give it a yank when I need it. I made it a few years ago when I first learned about trolls. I was with some experienced birders in southeastern Oregon where cattle share the open range with the birds. Cattle guards were built where the dirt road crossed a fence line. These are shallow pits with old railroad rails placed across them that allow cars to pass but not the cattle, which see the spaces and won't step on the rails. My friends were chatting in the front seat of the car while we were rumbling along to the next birding spot. Every time we approached a cattle guard, the conversation halted, they called out "toot, toot" in unison, and then continued as if that were a normal interjection.

Finally, I stuck my head forward to get their attention and asked, "What on earth are those toots for?"

"Oh, it's for the cattle guard trolls," Mike answered seriously. "They demand recognition from anyone who crosses over. If you don't pay them homage, they get pissed and you have bad luck."

Tooting seemed to work. We arrived at our next spot and discovered that one of the other cars had a flat tire. No one in the car had known about the trolls or their expectations and the trolls had their revenge.

Since I did not cross many cattle guards in the east, but did encounter inconsiderate drivers, the troll bell became part of a new ritual. When some driver did something rude, pick one, I rang my bell, wished them grace and let it go. I used it quite often.

I did not stop at Cape May, a popular birding spot. My book warned that parking was a challenge, so I added Cape May to my list of places to re-visit without Turtle.

One of my favorite books as a child was *Misty*, a tale about a pony that lived on the Chincoteague Wildlife Refuge on the barrier islands that stretch for 70 miles off the coast of Maryland and Virginia. My father's cousin, Posey Hurd, gave me the book when I was about seven. She was author of children's books herself and she knew I liked horses. I remember sinking into our living room couch next to her, with the book in my lap. While I turned the thick pages, Posey told me about a visit she made to Chincoteague while researching one of her own books about a boy who lived in a lighthouse. She timed her trip to watch the annual pony drive, an important element of the book she gave me. The ponies are rounded up and forced to swim across the channel to another island for a health check-up. If the herd has grown too large, a few of the ponies are sold. All very thrilling, she said, with the splashing and excitement of the ponies and people. In the story, Misty was the foal of one of the wildest mares on the island. The mare is captured for the first time in the history of the drive and two children buy them both with their summer berry picking money. The mare does not do well in captivity and is released, but Misty settles in so well that stories of her progeny appeared in subsequent books.

I looked forward to seeing the ponies in their wild state. Chincoteague Wildlife Refuge, the site of the book, occupies the southern part of Assateague Island but there is no camping on the refuge. However, there are facilities and ponies at Assateague Island National Seashore to the north, so I drove to the Barrier Island Visitor Center for maps, an update on the ponies and some history of the islands. Assateague and Chincoteague were the names of Indian tribes that lived in the area and met the first white settlers. The ponies live in two main herds divided by a fence at the Maryland/Virginia state line. The Chincoteague herd, Misty's herd, is still rounded up in July and many of the foals are sold at auction to support the volunteer fire department and to keep the herd at a sustainable size.

Leaving the visitor center, I crossed the high arching bridge onto the barrier island, a strip of sand between the Atlantic Ocean and Chincoteague Bay. Assateague Island is covered with dry grass, stumpy shrubs and short trees. I was disappointed when the herd didn't greet me, though I did see a sign that warned of the wild ponies that wander at will and can be dangerous. Great. Now where are they?

After claiming my camping spot, I set out to explore the long, skinny island. Barrier islands are built by sand pushed up by ocean waves, and are relatively flat, with dunes high enough to amuse small children who slide down their flanks. The islands are covered with tall oat grass, the major source of food for the horses though nutritionally inferior to mainland feed. Bayberry shrubs and pines hold onto the sandy soil between the ocean and Chincoteague Bay.

I drove to the ocean side and put on my hiking shoes. I saw the first wild horse after I tromped through the soft sand path from the parking lot to the beach. When I rose over the hump of the last dune and could see the ocean, I looked to my left to see a heavyset bay harassing a young couple who were snuggling in the shelter of the dune. It was a bit smaller than most horses but not the small pony I had expected, and it was behaving like an old barnyard plug begging for food and attention. It nudged the young man, who hesitantly reached out to pat its nose. Seeing no food, the horse snuffed and wandered off, and the young man lay back down on his blanket with his sweetie.

The hard sand beach was a pleasure to reach and I walked briskly to the north. When I returned I noticed a crowd of vehicles parked further down the shore, mostly pick-ups and SUVs. Tents and tables were set up next to them, and I could see a number of fishing poles stuck in the sand, their lines draped out into the ocean. People lounged in chairs and kids dug holes in the sand. A similar flat sand beach in Washington State is an important razor clam bed and vehicles are prohibited. Apparently no razor clams live on the ocean side of this island, but the surf fishing appeared to be good. Certainly the social aspect was lively.

When I returned to the parking area, I found a public car rinsing station, with pressurized air available to the drivers who had let out some air from their tires to get better grip on the sand. I thought the park was certainly accommodating to beach drivers in contrast to Oregon. I know of friends who drove out onto our beach, past the sign that indicated it was a bad idea, and got stuck. Even AAA wouldn't rescue them. Must be a different type of sand.

A brochure touted the clamming in Chincoteague Bay, popular as a sport and a business. Individuals are encouraged to find clams for their dinner using a tool like a garden rake, but with longer tongs. Clam diggers stand in knee-deep water, get a strong grip on the handle and force the rake into the sand. When the rake clanks against a clam, there's your dinner. The cherrystone clams have ribbed shells, similar to the ones I'd found with my toes in Mexico. The larger quahogs, another delicacy, live several inches under mud in other parts of the bay, and require a keen eye to spot the vent hole, and a strong shovel to dig into the heavy mud.

On my way back to Turtle, I found a small herd of the wild horses grazing around a large grass-covered roundabout. Several were bays, brown with black mane and tail. There was a black one with brown flanks and a white and brown pinto. Most of the horses were small but with big bellies, an adaptation to generations of their nutrition-sparse diet. Their bellies swell because they need to drink so much fresh water to overcome the effects of the salt in the grasses.

The horses looked so incongruous, doing their unhampered grazing, surrounded by people, cars, camping sites and restrooms. People drove carefully to avoid the animals that seemed to know they had the right of way. What a delight to see them running the show. From *Misty*, I knew the southern herd had the land to themselves, but this herd did not seem fazed by the presence of their adoring fans.

In one of the brochures, I read the sad story of a favorite old mare that got so habituated to cars, people and food that she stood in the road, begging, and was hit one evening by an unsuspecting tourist. Thus, the warning not to feed the horses. The danger to them is in their ease with people more than from their aggression. However, they were not always placid. A number of spectators watched the herd from a safe distance and a few were slowly creeping toward the peacefully grazing horses until the pinto mare laid back her ears and nipped the flank of a gray that jumped away from her. The people leaped back and resumed the properly respectful distance from these wild animals.

October 16, Virginia

The Chesapeake Bay Bridge-Tunnel connects the Delmarva Peninsula to the mainland at Norfolk, Virginia. The first section is a short solid bridge to Fisherman's Island, where I could see ducks sitting on the ponds, but there was no safe place to stop. A cruel fate for a birdwatcher. Back over the water, the highway had two lanes in each direction on separated concrete floats, safe enough for me to enjoy the view of the expansive bay and distant shore.

Suddenly, the four lanes merged to two and the divider disappeared. Trucks and cars raced towards me. The road dived down under the water, and the tunnel walls closed in. When trucks passed from the opposite direction in that restricted space, my ears compressed and popped. Then, zip, I was out in the open air again. I had been spit up onto a sunny mid-bay plaza with a restaurant and souvenir shop.

After breakfast there, I returned to Turtle to study my maps. A young gull teetered on the fence in front of me, staring and looking hopeful. Then I noticed a flock of unfamiliar birds settled down on the pavement right outside my window. They casually sidestepped to accommodate a car sliding into the slot next to me. I got out my books while the robin-sized birds fluffed and chittered sociably on the curb. They were probably shore birds, with stumpy, orange legs, short, pointed bills, and a distinctive calico pattern on their back. I found the shorebird section of my book and quickly discovered that my little companions perfectly matched the picture of ruddy turnstones in their winter plumage. Oh, yes. Another first. And I found them rather speedily. I was learning.

Pea Island National Wildlife Refuge, on the outer banks of North Carolina, is on another skinny strip of sand between the bay and sea. In *Kingbird Highway* by Ken Kaufman, who is now a well-known birder, I had read that he had gotten caught in an early snowstorm in the area and spent the night in his chilly car. I didn't think that was likely on that bright day.

I parked in the refuge lot. The sun was too high to see colors on birds well, but I wanted to try out my new book carrier I had purchased at the Assateague information center. Its pouch on a belt was much handier than carrying my bird identification book in my pack or a pocket as I had been doing. Now I faced the challenge of what books to carry, where to put my glasses, pen, my notebook. How tight should the strap be, snug or low slung? Hang it in front, side or back? All these things I had to work out to be a real birder.

When I felt properly dressed and adjusted, I crossed a short bridge over a little pond at the beginning of the trail. Turtles with lunch plate-sized shells were submerged, their noses snorkeling air. A bigger one, dinner plate size, slept under the bridge. I asked a young couple returning from the trail if they knew these kinds of turtles. In a strong southern accent, the young man said, "Well, I don't know those, but that big 'un is a snapping turtle. They're born mean and cranky. They hurt." I took his word for it.

The well-trod path between the two refuge ponds tunneled through stumpy, wind blown pines. After a hundred feet, it opened out onto the north pond. I spotted a flash of red in a bush near me. A cardinal! My heart jumped at his crimson body and his jaunty crest that wiggled when he turned his head. I masked my elation should any jaded easterners be watching. I'd seen cardinals on visits to the Midwest but that was before I noted sightings and we don't have any cardinals in my area.

A little further on, an elderly couple argued in good humor over the identification of a sparrow. Sparrows are one of the species I had put aside to learn later, when I ran out of the colorful birds. Jean and Bill introduced themselves and invited me to join them. I was pleased to recognize a few of the birds we saw, but they taught me new ones, like the palm warbler that lurked and twitted in the shrubs. I spotted a distant heron stalking along the edge of a small island in the pond, and Bill pointed out its white diaper, the distinguishing mark for a Tricolored Heron, common in their home territory of Texas and Louisiana.

I really needed their help to identify the lesser yellowlegs (very similar to the greater yellowlegs only a bit smaller). Positive identification relies on knowing the relative sizes of birds, and I had a long way to go before I developed that skill. It was apparent my companions did not need to refer to a book often because they didn't even carry one. I proudly offered mine, so handy in my handsome case, when Jean wanted to check some arcane point about another little brown bird.

I began identifying myself as a birder after my first five-day birding trip the previous May with an Audubon group. Since then I have been writing the date and place I first see a species of bird in my National Geographic bird book. If I am alone, I will err on the side of assuming the bird is common, but when I am with people like Jean or Bill, I can write in the data for a new sighting with greater certainty. I added several new birds as we strolled the dike. Seeing and noting each one was a thrill.

On the far side of the pond, we climbed a tower overlooking both ponds and scanned them from our perch, but there was not much to see that we hadn't already. The wind was piercing my thin jacket and the sun was setting, so I left Bill and Jean to heckle each other over another obscure point of identification and hurried back to Turtle.

Heading south, I passed communities of sturdy, beach houses of recent design, not shacks, and built at least ten feet up off the ground, with only posts and lattice underneath. At first I thought they were built high for the view, but then I read the next sign. I was on Hatteras Island. I remembered seeing the name in weather reports for the east coast. It is an area often hit by hurricanes. Maybe the houses were on stilts to protect them from high water and heavy winds.

It was difficult to imagine hurricane-high water on that pleasant day. One bank sign I had passed in the afternoon read 85 degrees, and the weather forecast for the next October day was for highs in the 70's, lows in the 50's. Hard to believe we were still in the hurricane season, which runs from June 1 to November 30. Birders like storms because it blows birds off course and into their locality. However, I feared they would have the same effect on Turtle and was happy with the pleasant day. I could find those exotic birds somewhere else.

I found a lovely cheapo place in Rodanthe. Turtle had a nice flat spot and there was a hot shower for me, all for only $12.50, including the extra for electricity for my refrigerator. I did not get a bay view, but I didn't need one. The people who had the waterfront spots were obviously regulars, and they were gathered in small groups around picnic tables, quietly watching the sunset over the bay. I was not going to be there long enough to make friends, which takes quite a while for me, but I felt I a shared mood with the sunset fans.

Back on the mainland of North Carolina the next day, the air was thick and heavy as I drove through the marshy coastal flats. I passed soybean fields, a few trailers, an occasional brick house and fields of fat, white heads of cotton on spindly stalks. Deep ditches lined the road, draining the lowlands for the crops. I was headed for Mattamuskett National Wildlife Refuge to see the tundra swans. When I arrived and scouted the large lake, I discovered they had not arrived for the season and there were no other birds to be seen.

Near the staff headquarters, I snacked in front of a light-colored, boxy building with an outdoor porch built right over the creek. A sign indicated it had been a spa in the thirties, but not for long, and it had been boarded up for years. I imagined one of those movie fades back to when the building sparkled, and Gatsby-dressed people wandered casually around, martini glass in hand, accompanied by soft music wafting from an open window.

No martini glasses that day.

Near Goldsboro, North Carolina I pulled off on an exit ramp to call for my messages. When I started rolling again, the left front wheel squeaked with every turn. I stopped and reviewed the maintenance work on Turtle. At one place, where I'd paid for a full service package that included the lube, they hadn't checked the tires. I'd had a long conversation with the manager after I'd asked him to have the crew put 50 lbs of air in the rear and 40 in the front. He said they couldn't do that on a passenger car, and turned to another customer. He wouldn't hear that I had an RV truck, not a passenger car. I finally gave up on him and walked out to ask the crew chief what *had* been done, to learn that they hadn't done anything to the tires at all. And I could see they hadn't vacuumed, another thing on the list I had paid for. So, what else did they omit? Why was my wheel squeaking?

Could it be a bad bearing or maybe it was the brakes wearing. I remembered a customer service phone number printed on the case for my door key. It was worth a try. A very attentive lady at a communication center somewhere understood my problem and called around to find a shop with a lift that would enable them to work on an RV, since Turtle was too high for regular car lifts. After three tries, she found a guy in Fayetteville who said it was probably the brake linings, down to the squeal bar or some such thing. He could take me the next day, and assured me I would be safe until then.

By noon the next day, I was on the road again with new brake linings and proud of my own resourcefulness.

In Hamlin, North Carolina, I really wanted a hot lunch in Mom's diner, but no such duck in this burg. I spotted a Piggly Wiggly, a name I hadn't seen since I was very young, and decided to aisle graze and reminisce. The store was just like my memory, with the same creaking floors and dated displays. When I was four, I had my shoplifting lesson at a Piggly Wiggly in Lake Oswego. Gum at eye level. I thought it had been put there for me and took the colorful package like my Mom was doing. When she found me later with a mouthful of the gum, she whisked me back to the store where I had to put the remains of my booty into the beefy hand of the manager, who suppressed a smile while I mumbled an apology. A timely but embarrassing lesson.

The Hamlin Piggly Wiggly did not have much to accommodate an instant lunch. I bought some very salty lean beef and had to dig into my stores for some rice cakes to go with it.

The parking lot was not the scene I wanted for lunch, so I fired up Turtle. As I waited at the exit, several trucks passed, piled with open crates of live chickens, their flapping white feathers pulled through the holes by the wind. Feathers filled the air behind the truck and it seemed to be snowing. Kentucky Fried Chicken on the hoof.

I found a nice park with a lake for my noon repast. Several men were hanging out, two at a picnic table, but no picnic, nor chess set either. Another sat on a bench. They seemed to be killing time, not enjoying the park, just sitting and staring. A sign hung on a nearby building: "Job Center". They stared at me for a while and then left. I wondered what the work situation was there in that small town. Did my presence make them uncomfortable, scare them off? I hoped not. I was the interloper. They lived there.

Sitting sideways in the driver's seat, my back against the window to see the lake, alert for birds, I heard a tap behind me. A bleary-eyed guy with several days' growth on his face, a well-worn T-shirt under a grubby jeans jacket, was making pleading hand gestures outside my window. I was alarmed at his actions and I didn't feel safe opening the window. It was not clear what he wanted, though I could guess.

I shook my head firmly and after two or three repeats, he gave up and wandered off. I felt sad that I had to be suspicious, yet knew my caution was not without good cause. That was a situation in which one of my male friends would have plunked himself down and struck up a conversation and learned all sorts of things about the area. I envied his freedom to make that kind of contact. I don't often attribute my shyness to being a woman, but in that situation, it certainly did have an influence.

I rumbled on down to the Carolina Sandhills National Wildlife Refuge in South Carolina. At the edge of a small parking area in the midst of the pine forest a trail sign promised a birdwatching blind somewhere in the distance. As I hitched on my book carrier, a young woman and pre-teen girl emerged from the woods. They said they hadn't seen much. Never mind, I thought. It was good for a walk.

The blind was a three-sided structure with a sloping roof surrounded by brush, typical of ones I'd sat in to watch unsuspecting birds at close range. This blind was near a small half-full lake. I sat down on the rough bench and peered out the slits. Not much on the pond, but I waited. Something moved to my right. I turned to find a little gray bird with a dark crest teetering on a twig not four feet from me. After studying it thoroughly, it remained as I pulled out my bird book and thumbed through it looking for birds with crests, not having another clue where to begin my search. I found it after the rather tedious process of flipping pages. An Eastern peewee. Another new bird for me. I felt so inept when all I could do was to look for crests. When would I be able to identify at least families to narrow my search?

No sooner had I logged him in my book than another little blue bird landed outside the left peephole. Its face and throat were black and its belly was white. A stunning black-throated blue warbler! It was easier to identify. At least I knew it was a songbird and once I found the warblers, picking out the markings was easy. It is one of the few birds whose name actually indicates what it looks like.

A more experienced birder told me that most birds were named when ornithologists shot the birds and studied the stuffed bodies. Sure, it's easy to see the ruby crown of the kinglet or the blue wing of the teal when you can handle the dead bird. Fortunately, we don't do that now and I felt lucky to see a blue bird with a black throat at such close range. Now, I'm willing to spearhead a movement to make what you can see at a distance part of the name.

At the next stop I pulled into a parking area next to a shady stream and turned off Turtle's ignition. On my first glance up into the trees, a medium-sized woodpecker with a bright red head scooted behind the tree trunk directly in front of me. I climbed out and waited. After a few minutes, he poked his head around the truck to see what I was doing. As he moved around I saw the black back with a big white patch on his rump to confirm that he was a red headed woodpecker, like in the cartoons. Excellent bird!

The next day I turned north and west again toward Great Smoky Mountains National Park. As I paid for my gas in Hendersonville, North Carolina, Rush Limbaugh ranted from the radio in the grubby office. I waited for the paunchy attendant to give me my credit card slip and kept my mouth shut. Another opportunity to discover tidbits of local news, but I was hungry and not in the mood for guarded chitchat.

For lunch, I wanted grease. My dinner the night before had been grapes, celery and peanut butter, ginger snaps and milk. I wanted meat. I joined the business crowd at Kelly's, an upscale restaurant. My hamburger was perfect, fat and juicy with a fresh bun. The cheese was tasty but did not overpower the meat. Heaven.

A table full of men and women in the center of the room caught my attention as they bowed their heads and held hands for a prayer after the plates were served. I heard "Scripture" mentioned several times but in the Bible belt I appreciate exposure to such conversations. During election season, when I puzzle about polling results that differ so much from my own opinion, I'll remember this scene and that these people are all seemingly normal and sane and not the demons I picture when I bemoan the state of the nation. We probably have a lot in common, and some things not.

Back on the road, I found an entrance to the Blue Ridge Parkway, which flows along the spine of the Blue Ridge Mountains in Pisgah National Forest still in North Carolina. The mountains are an older range than western mountains, lower and less rugged. Riding along those ridges, I felt like I was in a boat, rising to the crest of a wave and plunging down into the trough only to rise again. Oak and hickory forests in somber magenta, ochre and a few evergreens rolled away from the two-lane road. Cars were stopped at every viewpoint. I drove 100 miles or so on the parkway and scouted one campground that clung to the side of the mountain. The sites were appealing but primitive with no electricity. Fall mornings were brisk and I liked to be able to use my electric heater to take the chill off, so I returned to the road.

At the south end of the parkway the road dropped down and down, and it was easy to let gravity take over my descent, braking only as the turns became tight. At the bottom, I scanned the brochures at the Oconaluftee Visitor Center at the entrance to the Great Smokey Mountains National Park. I came across a warning to take care on the steep hills. Use low gear. Don't rely solely on your brakes. Oops.

I rushed back to the parking lot and felt Turtle's wheel hubs. Ouch! They were sizzling hot. Brilliant. New brake job yesterday, burn them out today, or warp the rotors, a term I'd just learned, or something else stupid. Well, at least I had new brakes, not the old ones. That would have really been pretty ugly if the brakes had given out.

There was also a notice that the nearby park campgrounds were full, so I turned south toward Cherokee, a town on the

Cherokee Indian Reservation that abutted the park. I found a commercial campground and pulled into my assigned site. The bulk of the sites were filled with semi-permanent residents, mostly retired couples, who had cheered their sites with flower boxes filled with bright red geraniums. They were enjoying the last weekend before the park closed for the season. Some were strolling around visiting friends; others were packing for their trek to warmer climates or hosting evening cocktails before pulling out. I envied their ease with each other, their familiarity. Once again I felt the limitations of my restless life on the road but I couldn't imagine living for a long period of time in a campground like this, with sites so close together and little privacy unless I closed my curtains.

October 20, North Carolina

The next morning at breakfast, I wrote in my journal, "I need to whine for a while. OK?" as if the trip shouldn't have its low spots. I'd opened my eyes at 4:30 a.m. but it was too early to get up. Park rules. No motors before 7 a.m. My mind wandered, and of course, I did not dwell on cheerful things, like how great a trip I was having and the fantastic birds, but how I could have severely damaged Turtle's brakes the previous day. Why wasn't I thinking about them during those free-fall moments I plunged down those hills? Well, I was listening to my taped book, that's why. Early on, I vowed not to listen to them except on freeways, so I wouldn't miss good scenery. I'd backpedaled a bit so I could listen when on a divided highway. But mountain roads were definitely off limits, except that day. I was bored. How many pretty trees and winding roads can one take? I wanted to get to the park to see a bit of it and find a campground. I was getting tired of the up and down and up and down. Oh, it did cross my mind how like the Wallowa Mountains in Oregon this was, where I did "learn" hill driving on the very steep road up to Hat Point. So steep, I used my lowest gear to grind my way up the road and even so, I had to stop and let the motor cool. Coming down, I used that same low gear to protect the brakes. I knew better than to ride the brakes all the way down. So, why not on the Blue Ridge Parkway? Because I was listening to my tape. Naughty me.

In the early morning I had a chance to rue my behavior, over and over. I would have been in even deeper trouble if I hadn't gotten the front discs replaced that very morning. But did I dwell on that? About how lucky I was that I had new brakes? No. I worried about what else could be on the edge. Tires. I'd get new ones when I got home. Could I make it? They were far from failing the Lincoln penny test, but does that mean they're still safe in heavy rain? It wasn't raining then, but surely I'd run into some rain before the end of the trip.

Should I get new tires now? And the joints. Have they been properly lubed? How many times has that been "lost" when I thought it was being done? Does Jiffy Lube do what is suggested in my maintenance book? Wal Mart screwed up. Who else did?

So, I worked on those things for an hour interspersed with thoughts of where to go that day. Gatlinburg was an hour away. I could do a little ancestor research in nearby Sparta. If I stopped halfway at some scenic overlook for breakfast and sunrise, I'd still have two hours to wait before any library was open. And then-and then . . .

Will I make my Los Angeles connection in November when I travel to another conference?

Now that was something I could do NOTHING about. GET A GRIP.

Another motor fired up, and tires crunched quietly down the road. I'd fallen asleep. It was 6:55. The sky had begun to lighten. Time to go. I got dressed, climbed into the driver's seat and crunched out on the gravel. At the intersection, a school bus had pulled half off the other side of the road, and a line of cars, released from following the bus, sped by in front of me. I was at an awkward angle, straining to see if anything was coming from the right after the bus-delayed line had passed. It was clear though there was a curve not far up the road. I was half way into the lane when a horn blared angrily and a zippy little red car whizzed between Turtle and the bus, going at a speed way too fast for that road. I swerved and missed it but my heart raced with surprise and shock.

I drove toward town feeling rattled and far from home. I didn't have my route for the morning plotted for certain. I wasn't in the mood for Sparta any more, nor did I want to tackle more hills. Maybe Alabama called.

At almost full light I found a haven in the café of a Best Western Motel in Cherokee. It was full of German tourists preparing for another day in America. There are lots of Best Westerns in the west and I felt I was in familiar surroundings and safe. Two eggs, toast, "home fries" (far from their home and mine), coffee and even o.j. Comfort food.

By the time I finished breakfast, I'd filled the pages of my journal with my woes and in black and white, they seemed more like a comedy than the tragedy they first seemed to be. The sun was out and the day was beautiful.

The winding mountain road that meandered west through the Nantahala Mountains on Highway 74/19 was designated a Scenic Byway on my map. In the friendly sunshine, the winding did not bother me. Signs were posted on trees in the Nantahala Gorge for several rafting companies. Flags planted in the streambed, which contained only a trickle of water, hinted of the frantic early spring, when the snow melts in the warm rains, the water is wild and kayaking is spectacular. I read that 150,000 summer people enjoy the more sedate river and the area is close to the Appalachian Trail, so tourists can hike through the natural beauty of the gorge. But on this fall day, the most of the tourists were at home.

As I left Nantahala on a narrow, winding road, a large truck zoomed up and passed me. Another cut me off as I entered a tight turn. Cars followed close enough to read my fuel gauge through the back window. I did my best to pull off and let them by, but there were not many safe opportunities. Then I passed a sign: "Share the road with bicyclists." Are they nuts, I yelled into the dashboard? Anyone cycling that road must have a death wish. This was *not* a scenic byway. It was a major arterial. Did the highway department put up signs designating roads like this to avoid having to find the money to straighten them?

No one answered. Turtle was a good listener.

This was not an isolated forest road, either, like mountain roads in the west. Houses, mailboxes and signs for small businesses indicated that many people lived in the area, on the roadside or down driveways that disappeared into the brush.

Mountain roads take attention I reminded myself. I did not put on an audiotape. I mulled over the signs instead.

"Prepare for death now. After you die, it's too late." Ha ha.

"Homecoming Oct. 5. We still pray" next to a high school. A chilling reminder of some problems regarding the separation of church and state.

"Cherokee Corn Maze". At first I thought Corn Maze was redundant, something that bugs me, like "descending down". Then I realized it was Maze, not Maize.

At least every mile there was a freestanding rectangular sign planted in a driveway. Same model each time, different message. Each sign was topped by a big arrow filled in with blinking light bulbs for emphasis, four on the shaft and three on the arrowhead. Below the arrow, the message, in curved snap-in letters with a background of yellowed plastic. "Yard sale" "Puppies" "Motor overhauls, cheap"

"1 mile to Aunt Suzie's Flea Barn." A flea circus or flea market in that barn? Or maybe there were rows of tiny stalls, one for each flea, boarders welcome.

"Boiled Peanuts" (I'd heard that pronounced "bold"). Several of those.

I'd love to meet the person who sold all those signs. He probably runs high-priced courses for salespeople now.

I rounded a turn and saw that a stack of smashed car bodies held up the road that skirted the next bend in the streambed. The ultimate in recycling.

Street names were another wonder asking for the story behind the choice:

"Granny Squirrel Gap Road"

"Worm Creek Drive"

And then there was "Kudzu Cable TV." A joke, yes? Make lemonade out of lemons, going with the flow? The kudzu vine was introduced to the U.S. at the 1876 World Exposition in Philadelphia in a Japanese exhibit. The large leaves and fragrant flowers intrigued gardeners. It was found to be good feed for livestock, and was planted in the southeast during the Depression for erosion control. Unfortunately, the climate was more favorable than Japan's for growing and the natural enemies were not imported along with the vine.

Kudzu can grow up to sixty feet a year, resists herbicides and is choking out the native plants. Southerners joke that they close their windows at night so the kudzu won't grow in. The reports were quite true. All I could see along the road was kudzu. Only lumps hinted of other plants under the thick mass of vines.

Over the mountains and back on a divided highway, my very favorite billboard showed two guys, one with a Viking's winged helmet, and both with really stupid expressions. "They vote. Shouldn't you?"

Perfect. I loved it.

I passed through a corner of Tennessee on Highway 74, stopped in Cleveland for my emails and took a short hike up an abandoned road. Then, I drove on to Alabama down I-59. In Fort Payne, Sock Capital of the World, I restocked my groceries. I passed up the Hosiery Museum and the Unclaimed Baggage Center (Remarkable Shops). I couldn't do everything and Little River Canyon N. Pres. looked more interesting. What is an N. Pres.?

The scenic drive was a narrow road that skirted the edge of a deep canyon. At the Little River Falls Overlook, I watched the thinnest of dribbles flowing over the lip of a sandstone cliff down several hundred feet into the canyon. A native son drove up with the wife in his car and climbed out.

"Howdy," he said. I nodded with a smile.

"Nice spot isn't it?" he went on. I agreed. "I came to check the leaves for a visitor who's coming soon." He paused and looked around. "Sorry about the lack of water. The waterfall is really spectacular, with more water."

Most are.

The road was a true Scenic Byway, chosen for its "landscape of high aesthetic value." There were only a few cars on this one in contrast the one outside of Cherokee. Unfortunately, two carloads pulled into the overlook where I was unsuccessfully waiting for birds, so I moved on.

At the next viewpoint, I was having a little pee in preparation for more bird watching when the two cars caught up with me. I was glad for my privacy door that preserved my modesty, but it seemed we were on the same tour. How unfortunate. Not that they weren't nice people, I'm sure, but it's hard to expect the birds to stick around when nice people scare them off.

I was beginning to see that the adventures I enjoyed most did not include people. Before the trip I had read *Blue Highways*, by William Least Heat Moon, where much of the charm of the book is in his conversations with people, finding out what they were thinking, what worried them, what made them happy? I'm sure he had to talk with many people before culling the best conversations, and that was not my idea of a pleasant time. I wondered how he could remember the dialects and nuances of speech until I read that he taped the conversations. Now that added way too much clutter to what I wanted to be a spontaneous adventure. I tend to mull them over after climbing back into Turtle, which is why I am left with unanswered questions. I could never think fast enough in the moment to generate all the questions I might be able to conjure up later, and besides, they wouldn't come in a linear sequence, anyway.

No, my style is more of a voyeur. I watch and listen and muse. It's like unraveling a puzzle. If you have the answer to begin with, where's the challenge? What is there to fill the time once I'm back on the road? Not that following a line of questions with someone doesn't lead to unexpected answers, but they then cancel out the other intriguing possibilities. Kind of like the way I explore the countryside. If I know exactly where I'm going and choose the shortest route, I miss what I might have discovered by a more circuitous path, including the destination. My proposed daily destinations are really to help me decide which way to make my first turn. After that, it's all open to outside influences. So, my interactions with people tend to be fuel for my imagination after I've learned all the facts in the moment.

Alone again at Hawks Glide View Point, I peered down into the canyon. Trees blanketed the canyon walls and the river glinted through leaves that were beginning to turn. I was traveling faster than the seasons. Tan and striated rock faces popped out of the foliage on the other side of the gorge. No wind. No eagles gliding.

I continued south because the road went that way. N. Pres. it turned out, was a Natural Preserve, and it was truly lovely, but it was late afternoon and it was time to find a place to stop for the night. I looked for something that might pinpoint my location. The campground I'd spotted on the map was to the west of the interstate. I was to the east and headed south with no roads intersecting that might take me in the right direction. I was growing anxious.

The sky tried to be blue, but something took the color out of the middle and the orange sun hid behind it. The previous night, the sun had sunk into the horizon in a flair of red orange, the same color I remembered from the skies near Los Angeles, where I went to college. There in Alabama, there was a daily pattern of fog in the morning, a little sun, and then the smog, thanks to coal-fired electric plants and thermal inversions.

I finally got back to I-59 and took the next exit to the state park. The tiny directional signs were elusive, and after an anxious half-hour, it was pitch dark. Where the road became a gravel farm track, I stopped to get my bearings. A fenced field to my left. Trees that fell away down a hill to my right. Was I lost again?

I scanned the tree trunks and fence posts for another sign, but saw none. My maps were no help. All I could tell was that the campground was supposed to be in a canyon two miles north of Oak Grove. Then I noticed a very narrow paved road that plunged down into the trees. Nothing assured me this was a public road and that I would not find myself in someone's driveway at the end as in the movie, "The World According to Garp". What else was there to do? I turned Turtle onto the road and urged her forward, holding my breath, until I could actually see the road in the headlights. In low gear to save the brakes and maintain control, I wound down to the valley floor. At the end of the dark tunnel of trees, the road flattened and my headlights picked out a sign: Buck's Pocket State Park. Whew.

I pulled up to the deserted office to check for instructions and fees on the message board. A handwritten note directed an incoming group to the group camping area. I wondered if they had arrived. Most public campgrounds set up the group camp away from the other sites so a bunch of kids or partying adults would not disturb the rest of the camp. I listened for a ruckus but heard nothing, so if the group had arrived, they were far enough away for me to be happy.

I drove around the camping loop and found only four or five sites occupied. Two people stood next to a tent in the halo of illumination from their gas lantern, finishing their dinner clean up, and the rest of the people were inside their trailers and campers. No sign of a bunch of kids. I chose a site for maximum privacy, as far from the other campers as possible. I backed in, pleased with the isolation.

I thought by then I'd seen all kinds of showers. Here, three curtainless shower stalls opened onto the dressing area, but the one naked bulb in the room illuminated only the furthest stall. Naked and chilly, I reached in to turn on the water to find there was only one make-do faucet handle, bright red. I flipped it on and jumped back, expecting the initial cold rush of water. Boiling steam filled the stall. My tired brain grappled for a way to bathe without cooking myself. Lobsters came to mind. I managed to shut off the steam vent and groped my way into one of the darkened stalls. I could feel the two handles in the dark and pushed aside thoughts of what else might be in there with me.

By 8 o'clock, I was cozy, clean and fed and writing in my journal when a pickup drove slowly by. Then another, followed by a parade of cars and pickups. Ten minutes later, the line of vehicles returned, having completed the loop around all the campsites. Two sites to my right they all pulled in and parked haphazardly. Shadows and flashlights moved in and out of the headlights as they unloaded the vehicles. Kids spread out and filled the area between the tree trunks where there were no bushes or boundaries to define the different campsites. It sounded like a schoolyard at recess next door: shouts, laughter, a few adult voices, snapping towels and loud laughs. Several Coleman lanterns were hung in the trees and tents popped up after lively discussions.

Chattering pre-teens wandered past me in small groups on their way to the shower building. Good. They are brushing their teeth and off to bed, I thought.

I was such an optimist.

Several kids crunched across my gravel pad. *My* pad! I tried to relax and retreated to my curtain-private bed for solitude. I read a little, and then, hoping they were moving toward lights out, I peeked under the curtains. There were still lots of lights moving around in the trees and some laughing. A tarp was unfolding next to the vehicles. I watched with a mixture of voyeuristic curiosity and curmudgeonly irritation.

I dozed off. When I awoke at 10:20 p.m., the camp seemed quieter. In the far campsite I saw a tarp big enough to cover an army held up with thin posts. Ten gas lanterns lit up the camp kitchen. I saw shadows carrying plates, making eating gestures.

After dinner the volume rose while the kids horsed around, playing some game with lots of pre-adolescent chicken-cackle laughing. Most campgrounds have quiet hours from 10 p.m. to 7 a.m. I guess their parents hadn't read the rules.

I dozed again and awoke to a quiet camp. I listened, ever

hopeful, but soon the kids returned from wherever they had gone, bringing back their laughing and yells.

At last, the voices seemed to be making their way to the washroom again. By midnight, the camp was finally quiet.

I drove out at daybreak, past the mega-campsite with 13 cars and 20+ tents. In daylight I could see South Sauty Creek that rimmed the campground. We were in a narrow gorge cut into the Sand Mountains and flanked by heavily wooded canyon walls.

Turtle ground her way up the steep entry road and followed a sign to a viewpoint. I parked in a pullout that seemed rather primitive but the view was good enough for breakfast. The orange-red sun rose behind me and tinted the thick haze that obscured most of my view. Over coffee, I watched the haze dissipate, revealing the tops of hills that stretched in waves to the west, like a traditional Japanese mountain scene.

What was down that road? Maps were no help, but as I was packing up, an old car passed from that direction, so I drove on.

A quarter of a mile further, I found The Jim Lynn Overlook Area, the real viewpoint, and it was well developed with a proper parking lot, picnic tables and a trail into the trees. The man in the car must have slept there since the road ended in the parking lot.

The trail began with a short set of wooden stairs and a sign: "Permit to rappel must be obtained at the park office."

Of course. Those steep walls of granite were perfect for rock-climbers. One of the paths threaded through the brush to the edge of a vertical wall where the dirt was packed hard. I peered over the lip, and at the base of the forty-foot drop, the dirt was well trampled where the climbers landed.

During my short rock-climbing career, I remember backing down a cliff, trusting my life to the person tied to a tree by a static rope. The rope that held me wound around her waist, and she let it slip slowly through her hands as I moved away from her and over the cliff. Backing off any cliff makes my heart race, regardless of what is below but once the wall is in front of my face, the descent is quite a thrill. And with the right gear, I'd do it again right on this spot.

The trees growing on the narrow bluff had been used as the anchor points to tie the safety person for the rappels. Roots rippled along the surface, their little tree-finger nails gripping every available crack. I picked my way over the roots for a hundred feet to the fenced overlook. Shrieks of the awakening scouts pierced the quiet morning from the campground below me. I pulled the crumpled brochure for Buck's Pocket State Park out of my pocket to review why I had come. "Unique Canyon Scenery" yes, "Botanical Growth" what isn't trampled, yes, "Peace and Tranquility", well, maybe another time.

In case the days' calendar for the troops included rappelling, I got outta there.

October 21, Alabama

Jack's Fast Food served the Deluxe Breakfast on a paper plate with one large and two small pockets: light yellow scrambled eggs, two sausage patties, a large white floury biscuit, hash browns (coated sticks deep fried), one pocket of white corn grits with a big squirt of butter dripping off the side and one pocket overfull of white gravy with chunks of something in it. Some color would have livened it up. It was WAY more than I could have eaten if I had been really hungry, which I wasn't, but now I knew what "The Jack's Big Breakfast" was.

Not much driving that day because I had to stay the night in Mississippi to add it to my collection. I didn't have far to go to find Tishomingo State Park, named after a Chickasaw chief. It was a popular camping spot that weekend and cheap: twelve dollars. The camping areas were nicely treed with hardwoods and with light underbrush. Older couples sat chatting next to their big rigs. The lake was very low, mostly caked mud and stumps.

When I shut off the motor at an empty lakeside site, I could hear the chatter of kingfishers as they zoomed across the water. On the tree right next to me, a white-breasted nuthatch crept down the trunk. It glanced at me and then went back to looking for bugs in the bark. A good sign. I liked it there.

On my bike ride that hot and humid afternoon, I passed a poster on a bulletin board that gave me a clue about some of the other visitors. "Welcome dulcimers." Players of, I assumed. Some kind of gathering, but no performance. I had the feeling the musicians were clustered in the trailers, learning tunes and techniques from each other. Later, on my way to the shower, I strained to hear the mellow dulcimer chords, but had no luck.

The park is in the northeast corner of Mississippi, close to Alabama and Tennessee. The conversations I overheard contained thick-extra syllables: yay-es, thank yeeuw among slow, drawn out sentences. Overhearing a just few snippets of conversation slowed me way down.

I watched the light fade and thought about the next day. I planned to stay near Memphis, Tennessee, the last state for my collection. A wash of anxiety swept over me. THEN WHAT? Then I relaxed. What does it matter what we seek as long as the seeking bears the rich fruits of experience? Is it the quarry or the hunt? The journey or the destination? For me, it's the journey. Silly lists take me off the tourist routes. My first collection was of the 36 county seats in Oregon. After that, I took less than two years to visit and collect all 256 incorporated cities and towns in my home state. I may be the only person with photos of every one.

Maybe the next quest would be for birds. My new bookcase would make it so much easier in the field. I felt very jaunty wearing it, if I did say so. The hunt for new birds could cover lots of new places.

Early the next morning was hot and humid again. On my hike I felt as if I was swimming through warm molasses. Even so, I sighted two new birds, an eastern bluebird and a blue jay, and wondered why I had not seen them sooner since they are common all over the east. Well, besides finding a birdy area, serendipity is an important element to success.

After another shower, I pulled Turtle onto the Natchez Trace, which runs right through the state park. On the map, the fat green line of the Trace runs southwest to northeast, from Natchez, Mississippi to Nashville, Tennessee. I remembered an old article in National Geographic, showing an old cart track under heavy trees. One picture showed a six-foot deep groove dug into a hillside by the carts. I wanted to drive a bit of it to get a sense of the history even though it would not advance me on my westerly path.

The trace was originally a trail made by bison and followed by Indian hunters. In the early 1800s, treaties with Chickasaw and Cherokee Indians provided for the opening of a wagon road from Nashville to Natchez. After the Mississippi River became a commercial conduit for goods, men who worked the cargo boats down to Natchez walked the trace back to Tennessee. A paved road of 440 miles parallels the recently restored path.

Driving on the quiet, flat two-lane road was a joy. A mowed-grass shoulder sloped slightly down to a row of pines and maples. Occasionally, the trees gave way to fields and a farmhouse. No advertising, no stop signs, no trucks, no one pushing from behind. At crossroads, I glided up and over to other road on a berm. Occasionally, a quiet junction with a small sign indicated there was a town somewhere close by, but none could be seen from the trace. I stopped frequently at historic sites: the remains of an old farm, store or mine or a noted battle site or migration trail. I was often the only person in the little parking areas.

Bear Creek Mound at milepost 308.8 was a flat-topped grassy mound, originally built between 1100 and 1300 A.D., determined by archeologists dating the mud plaster found in construction on the site. The original mound was for ceremonies or an elite home but had been plowed and lowered in recent times. The Park Service restored it to the original estimated height of eight feet high, 85 feet across the base.

While I was musing on the history, a young family parked in the lot. An energetic little boy jumped out of the car and ran for the mound. He struggled up its sloped side and, once on top, yelled to his parents. With all eyes on him, he flopped onto the grass and rolled down the ancient grassy slope, shrieking with pleasure.

Sunken Trace, Tennessee, milepost 351, was an area where the original trail got mushy and the wagons returning upriver detoured into the brush. Then the new trail got mushy and eventually the area was covered with a wide selection of routes. Following the path into the woods, I crossed three gouged ruts. The deepest was a gash six feet deep in places overhung by a canopy of trees. It cut through the crest of the hill and I looked up to see that the bottom of the cut was as round as the bottom half of a pipe. I was astonished to realize this was the place in the picture I remembered.

Sunken Trace is one of the remnants of the original trace, and back in the trees, I could imagine the creaking ox-drawn wagon or the footfalls of rugged merchants returning to Nashville. Practical men, the merchants would build a heavy flatboat upriver, load it with their merchandise, and float it down to Natchez. Once the goods were sold, they disassembled the boats, sold them for lumber and walked home along the Natchez Trace to begin again. They crossed rivers, bogs and marshes, and had to be alert for snakes and bears as well as for bandits eager to separate them from their new wealth.

The modern version of the Natchez Trace had no rest stops WITH sanitary facilities, and unfortunately, shrubs around the Sunken Trace seemed especially well littered with brown striped paper. Where is the logic in that? Didn't the planners ever travel with children?

When I returned to Turtle after gingerly exploring the old ruts, a newly arrived three-generational family was unloading from their family van. A stocky old duffer said to his grandson of about four, "Here. Papa's going to make you a snake stick." He pulled the leaves off a long, straight branch and gave it to the boy, who dutifully plunged down the dirt path, waving the stick side to side to scare off whatever wildlife awaited him and his family. I could have mentioned that I hadn't seen any snakes, but that would have spoiled his fun. Then again, maybe I was too blasé. Maybe I was lucky I hadn't come across one of the snakes. I know how to deal with rattlesnakes, but there are some in the south that are as poisonous, like copperheads and coral snakes, and they don't have the courtesy to rattle before striking.

I left the trace at the next exit. Once off the well-groomed park road, I passed rundown farmhouses and several cemeteries that seemed to be celebrating perpetual Memorial Day. Every tombstone supported a huge bouquet of faded plastic flowers.

At Daniel's CeeBee Grocery in Collinwood, Tennessee, I tried another experiment: I bought a bag of "put a little south in your mouth Pork Rinds." I popped one of the fried tidbits in my mouth. Salty. Porky. Like puffy potato chips. Then I chewed it a few times and my saliva didn't have much impact on the solid ball of fat that it became. I tried a sip of water, but when I swallowed, the greasy lump went down about three inches and quit moving. A big gulp pushed it on down. I passed up future pleasures and threw away the rest of the bag. Must be an acquired taste.

Stopped for traffic in the exit from the CeeBee Grocery parking lot, Turtle straddled a drainage ditch. On the pavement down to my left sat a six-inch tortoise poised for action. His little head looked right and left as if waiting his turn to cross the exit road where Turtle was idling. I looked back the way he must have come, but there was only the ditch in the grassy side of a busy street. I jumped out and moved him to the ditch on the opposite side and hoped he would survive.

I had seen another tortoise beside the freeway the previous day as I flew by two feet from his nose. But I've never seen a flattened one. Do they really know when to cross?

More signs on churches: "If God is Your Co-Pilot, Swap Seats." I don't understand the reference. And there were a lot of Primitive Baptist churches and I'd never heard of that sect. I checked their web site, which explains that the name conveys the idea of originality and simplicity. They stick close to the original interpretations of the scriptures and do not accommodate societal norms. Something new every day.

Later, I drove through devastated forest land: clear cut, poorly cleaned and not replanted, ragged and ugly, yet the houses in the area were reasonably well kept. I was approaching Savannah, Tennessee, leaving the fields behind, when I noticed something odd. On a section of the tree lined road, several very large gates flashed by. The entry gates usually incorporated an arch or stone pillars and had long fences on both sides made of wrought iron or wooden planks, but at the end of the property, the fence simply ended. It didn't surround the property, only the face of it. So what was it for? It reminded me of men who sit in a restaurant and inch the cutlery away from them to define an ever-larger space for themselves. A power play, a leadership trainer said once. Do the fences say: this is mine? Then what? Stay out? Nope. You could go around. Probably the message is: "Eat your heart out. It's all mine."

That night was the big night. At Fuller State Park in Memphis, Tennessee, I marked my fiftieth state. But, I didn't take the time to celebrate. I was on to another search: birds, seriously, now.

October 23, Tennessee

In the morning, I got up early, anticipating an easy drive to the T.E. Maxon Wastewater Treatment Facility, a prime birding site according to my book. I would have thought a wastewater treatment facility would not be hard to find, but the direction witch struck again. The road I was following ended at a T-intersection with a state highway and I still had a mile to go. No indication that it continued several hundred yards down that highway, but I finally figured it out.

I found the administrations building, but didn't see any ponds. The book said to ask permission. The door to the building was open so I walked in, listening for voices but hearing none. In a tiny room in the back, I found a live person, a man who was totally mystified about my quest, as if no other birder had ever been there. He called Charlie at maintenance and gave me directions to the shop across that disruptive highway.

At the maintenance yard, well-padded Charlie drove up with his skinny helper in the cab of his pickup.

"You the gal who wants to see our birds?" Charlie said pleasantly.

"I sure am. I hear you have a great site here."

"Sure do. Hop in. I'll show you around so you don't get run down by the trucks."

Charlie introduced me to his assistant, a much smaller man than Charlie, thankfully, who hopped out so I could get in between them. They drove me on a tour around dikes that enclosed the sewage ponds, huge square sheets of thick, green water. He showed me where to see the birds and pointed out the roads the monster trucks hauling dried sewage would be using so I could avoid them. Charlie was very hospitable and wanted to give me all the details.

"You know, we sure see a lotta birds here. A lotta guys come to look at them, too. Groups, usually. Bring their binoculars and sometimes those big telescopes, even."

"I found you in my book that shows where to find the birds in this area. It's no wonder birders come here."

"Yeah, well, I sure wish they'd teach us the names. We see birds every day, and we know which ones are passing through. Kinda hard to keep track when we don't have names for them," he said wistfully.

I pointed out the few I knew. What Charlie really needed was for someone to tutor him on identification and to encourage him to report when unusual birds flew in. I knew of birders at home who kept records, tracked breeding areas and migration trends, and find the rare birds blown off course. Charlie would have liked to meet their peers in Memphis.

Charlie was a slow talker, so slow I kept finishing his sentences for him, and then bit my tongue at my gaff. Minutes later, I'd do it again. He didn't seem to notice.

After our tour, Charlie dropped me off and I drove Turtle around to the pond with the most birds. I parked under some trees on the dike and lowered my side windows for a clear view of the green wing teal, killdeer, snipe (a first), mallards, and red tailed hawks. Many ducks dabble by tipping up and paddling with their feet to keep their heads down into the weeds searching for food, and I'd seen shovelers doing that as well. The water seemed to have some kind of scum or duckweed on the surface and for the first time I saw shovelers feed by gobbling their extra-wide bills built for that purpose across the surface.

After eyeing all the birds for a good while, I moved down the dike to write in my journal, away from the flies. I left my windows open, hoping the flies that had joined me would leave. They didn't. They liked the shade and settled in. Two of them stayed with me for two more days. They were more like traveling companions than an annoyance. They didn't bite, and usually stayed in a corner while I ate. Two days later, I opened Turtle wide for a good cleaning and they left. I almost missed them.

After leaving the sewage ponds, I took off on Highway 40 across Arkansas. I'd visited Arkansas the year before, so I didn't plan an overnight in that state.

On the previous trip, I was hunting for a mill my great-grandfather Matt Smith had once partially owned. From his letters I knew that as a young man, he started a retail lumberyard in Thayer, Kansas. By being extremely frugal during difficult times he had cash to lend to his suppliers during the Depression lest they go out of business. Some did anyway, and he ended up owning part of Rosboro Lumber, an Arkansas company. This tidbit of information was only remotely interesting to me, since Matt Smith probably didn't have a lot of personal investment in the community, but it was a hook for some explorations.

I had rooted around in the library in Hot Springs, Arkansas hoping to find some clues about the company and discovered that a tiny town of Rosboro was still on the map. The closest town of any size to it was Glenwood, so I hopped in Turtle for the short drive.

I asked at the library and newspaper office for anyone who might have information and was given a number for Mrs. Sam Adams, who knew all the history of the area, and called her on a pay phone. She lived within sight of the phone and would love to tell me about Rosboro.

Across the street, blue-haired, slim and well dressed Mrs. Adams met me as I walked up her flower-lined path. Her well-kept white house and tidy yard fit so well in the old town, two-story with a wide front porch with a little brick-a-brac around the overhang.

"It's so nice to meet you. It's not often I get to talk about Rosboro because everyone here knows as much as I do," she said and invited me to sit on the sunny porch. Over lemonade, she and her husband told me fascinating details I could never remember, though little was about my ancestor. Half the town of Glenwood had worked and lived in Rosboro. Maybe more, since so many of the people we could see from the porch seemed to be older, the younger ones having moved on, she said.

Then she offered to give me a tour, agreeing to meet her husband at the senior center for dinner when we were done. We climbed in her Lincoln and putted down the road for a few miles. She pointed out the old mill site, where the log pond still had some water in it, but the mill had been torn down leaving a wide, flat area now weeded over. The manager's house still stood nearby and was occupied, but most of the other housing of the town had been demolished. But, she said, the town was on the upswing with the new high school, built between two more populous towns that shared the facility, and she felt Rosboro would revive soon. The mill was the center of a close-knit community and Mrs. Adams enthusiastically described the activities among the families of workers: picnics, softball, community meetings, mutual support and emergency aid when needed.

But times change, she said. When the trees were all cut in the thirties, many of the families moved to Oregon, following the work. There were probably some descendants living in my home state now.

Then she asked if I would like to join her and her husband for dinner, my lunch, at the retirement home they helped establish. I gathered that they were generous philanthropists in that small town, and very proud that they had help with the construction of the building, though she assured me many times that they really lived in Texas now. I wondered why.

"We try to join them at least once a week, we know so many of them. Quite a number worked at the mill, and you can ask them about it."

It was interesting, but that type of situation is not my forte. Thanks to my hosts, who asked questions that had not occurred to me, we chatted mainly about Oregon relatives, or even places where some of them had once lived in Oregon, familiar to me as logging towns now as shriveled as Rosboro.

The whole experience was unusual for me. I left feeling a little guilty for taking up so much of her time, but she certainly didn't seem to mind, in fact seemed eager to share memories. I didn't quite know whether or how I should respond, but I had her business card so I could send her a note.

By the time I reached Oklahoma late in the day, I was tired of driving. Exiting the highway, I was looking for signs to Tenkiller State Park. Under the sign at the offramp was another one pointing to Sequoyah Wildlife Refuge in the opposite direction from Tenkiller. The afternoon was young enough, so I turned toward the refuge to investigate.

I parked Turtle next to the information kiosk for the refuge and spotted a promising dirt road that plunged into a lightly wooded area bordering a creek. I grabbed my book and binoculars but didn't change into my hiking shoes, thinking I wouldn't stay long.

I crept down the road, looking for birds and listening. A familiar call grabbed my attention and a woodpecker flashed into a high branch. I kept my eye on it as I tried to get into a better position to see. Suddenly, I stepped off one of those three-inch cliffs that seem like ten feet. Off balance, I teetered and planted the other foot. Cold oozed into my shoes. I looked down into a thick mud pit. Deal with the mud or the birds? Another woodpecker flew in, and not the same kind, it seemed. Never mind the shoes. Pull out the book. I tried to extract my feet without making any slurping noises, which might have scared off the birds. They stuck around long enough for me to get a tentative identification, a ladderback and a red cockaded woodpecker. That was a great spot.

I slogged on down the road, and saw some more birds I had recently identified. It was nice to reinforce my new knowledge. To return to Turtle, I chose the track that rimmed a fallow field. As I scanned overhead to follow another woodpecker, a different, heavier noise came from the base of the tree. I crept closer. Through the brush, I saw a scaly rounded surface, flexible as leather and the size of a large football. A pointed snout and twitchy ears pushed through some leaves. It was an armadillo! He poked and snuffled in the fallen branches and leaves, quit uninterested in me. In that area, armadillos are common as dirt, but seeing one was a thrill for me. I tried to watch both the armadillo and the bird, not very successfully, but I did stand still to avoid another fiasco. Oh, the richness of nature.

My shoes were disgusting when I got back to Turtle and the socks were a loss, but I didn't care.

Tenkiller State Park finally materialized, but no thanks to the crummy signage. I almost left the state, driving down several country roads trying to find the park. I swear I've got to get my signage and directions consultancy going. I could make a fortune.

I chose an isolated space for my night's repose and was writing in my travel log when a scruffy guy about forty approached. I was a little worried but it was daylight. He had on an old black T-shirt with rolled sleeves and biker boots and jeans. It was the scraggly beard that put me on edge. Then he pulled out a fee book and I relaxed.

As he handed me my receipt he said, "Watch out at night. Better carry a light. There's skunks around. They get into the garbage, and you don't want to run into one of them."

After a walk down by the lake and around the deserted picnic area, I considered dinner. From my site, I looked across an expanse of empty camping sites and grass to the public road and saw a little restaurant/gas station/store that looked open. It could be good for local chatter. However, by the time I would have finished my meal it would be pitch dark, and no meal was worth a skunk-fumigation, so I rummaged around in Turtle's stores and made do.

October 24, Oklahoma

I drove to Greenleaf State Park the next morning hoping for more birds. In a parking lot next to the lake, I relaxed with a second cup of coffee when there was splash to my left. I caught movement near the boathouses out of the corner of my eye and turned to see an osprey fly away with a fish wiggling in its talons. It is always a thrill to see birds catch their prey, but I'd seen ospreys at home. Minutes later a ranger drove up next to me, windows down.

"Did you see the osprey grab that fish? Right over there. Just a moment ago," he said, a little breathless. When the staff gets excited, it's worth noting. I didn't realize the importance of the event until I looked in my bird book. Ospreys are not supposed to be in Oklahoma. I had been enjoying seeing southeastern birds, but I didn't know what birds belong where. If I saw it, I saw it. Finding one where it does not belong is yet another layer of birding I needed to learn.

I wondered about the birds I'd seen the day before and checked my book. Oops. The ladder-back was not native to the southeast. The black and white ladder-like pattern on its back was not so distinct that I might have really seen a red-bellied woodpecker, noisy and numerous in the southern woods. And the red-cockaded woodpecker is very rare and only found in pine forests, which did not describe where I'd been. Oh, well. I'd enjoyed watching the birds, whatever they were.

I climbed out and moved to sit on the grass under some trees. In only a few minutes, a loud piliated woodpecker flew close in to attack an old log in the middle of the grassy area. Those woodpeckers are more often heard than seen, so I froze. I relaxed when he left, and in a tree above my head I found another eastern bluebird and my first Carolina chickadee. The difference between the Carolina and black-capped chickadees is subtle, a clean or ragged edge to the bottom part of the bib. More importantly, black-capped chickadees are not normally found in eastern Oklahoma, and Carolina chickadees are. I could learn this stuff yet.

Four men in country clothes were chatting in a genuine old-time café in Vinita, Oklahoma where I stopped for lunch. They were spread over two scarred wooden booths and one battered table, but they might as well have been sitting together, the way the conversation flowed. They were talking guns when I walked in. A slim guy, early thirties, sat at the table in the middle of the room, a nearly clean platter in front of him. He was turned half around in his chair to face two guys in a booth and said, "Yeah, I got four guns. They pretty much do all I need." His lip twitched with a sly smile. The others responded as if they had heard that line before: deadpan, no surprised laugh, accepting his humor.

Then they got onto kids.

The middle-aged guy in another booth by himself said, "When my kids need punishment they get barn duty."

"Zat so."

"Yep. Gotta clean the barn. I gotta do it every day. Those kids get off easy so I make'em get out there and pick up a shovel for a while." He paused. "They'd rather be whupped, but I don't give them that choice." Another pause. "The school counselor interviewed a bunch of kids about how they were treated when they did something wrong. She told me that barn duty was one of the most effective punishments she'd heard of. The kids hate it so much, they don't misbehave much any more."

These guys weren't quite what I expected in Oklahoma.

The waitress, cotton dress, beige apron and scuffed sneakers, burst out of the kitchen with platters and side dishes lined up her arm for the booth of two. She paused dramatically in the doorway so they would see the disgusted look on her face and announced, "Bad turkey." No one flinched. "Had to throw it out. God, it stunk," she added in the silence her announcement created.

I glanced down at the Reuben sandwich in my hand: sauerkraut, heavily preserved beef, rye bread, and pickles. I was safe. She slid the platters onto the table, and the men dug in. Apparently, they had not ordered turkey, either.

As I was finishing up, an older woman with big hair pushed through the door. Mrs. Big Hair may have been the mother-in-law of the waitress, from their conversation. She got the turkey story.

"Well, Earlene, you don't wanna tell everybody that. They don't wanna know all that goes on back there," chided Mrs. Big Hair.

The men reiterated their gun stories for her and she bragged about her sharp shooting prowess, citing several skeet shooting prizes. I lost the train of conversation as I paid my bill. When I looked up, the cook's assistant came out from the back, an older guy in a washed-thin T-shirt and a thick apron tied under his potbelly.

"Now that one. I'd pay a quarter for him," she said.

They all laughed. What had I missed? Drat.

By late afternoon, I rumbled into Chanute, Kansas, home to my Cousin Bill. I discovered Cousin Bill a few years ago while doing genealogical research. I had missed meeting him on my visit the previous fall, but this time he was expecting me. We had corresponded for several years trading information about our common ancestors. Bill retired from the military to the town where his family has lived for three generations, and he has the same name as his grandfather, so he was easy to find on the Internet white pages. The various degrees of cousinhood are beyond me, but our common ancestor is Benjamin Franklin Smith, my great great-grandfather and Bill's great-grandfather. In his letters, Bill told me to call him Cousin Bill, which saves having to figure out the links.

My great-grandfather, Matt Ryan Smith was born in 1866, the youngest son of Benjamin Franklin Smith, a railroad lawyer and alcoholic who died young, leaving his wife with seven children in Decatur, Illinois. By the time Matt and his mother Emily arrived in Galesburg, Kansas, south of Chanute, Matt was the only child still with his mother. How they arrived there and why is a mystery. It is possible they moved to the area because Matt's married sister, Fanny, lived in nearby Chanute.

I knew that Matt had worked summers in nearby Thayer at a lumberyard where he was taken on full time, right out of high school. He married his high school sweetheart when he was 20, and my grandfather was their firstborn. In 1887, Matt's sister Fanny, who was six years older and married to William Gray, persuaded her husband to loan Matt the Gray family savings to help him start his own lumberyard. Fanny was a great saver of everything, and Cousin Bill had all the letters my great-grandfather wrote to the Grays as annual reports during the years his loan was outstanding on stationary headed "Gray and Smith, Dealers in Lumber and Grain, Galesburg, Kansas."

The letters Bill had transcribed and sent to me were full of lumber and grain prices, business opportunities and failures, and some personal insights. In his first business report of August, 1887, Matt Smith wrote:

> My Dear Will: I wrote you a letter two weeks ago but let it lie around here for a few days and then burnt it. Had the blues when I wrote it so I put off answering your letter until I should have taken stock. I have just finished that job and enclose a report of our first half year's business.
>
> We can congratulate ourselves on the result.
>
> Crops are worse than they were last year, much worse in the vicinity of Galesburg especially. I can't see anything but hard times for another year to

> come but hope we can manage to make expenses. I can get along with less stamps and stationery . . .
>
> Lillie and Ralph are both well. The little boy is as little trouble as any baby I ever saw. My expenses on his account was about $40 and I owe about $20 yet which I hope to pay this quarter.

The little boy, Ralph, was my grandfather. In the next letter, February, 1888, I learned Matt's prediction of hard times proved correct:

> We can congratulate ourselves that (business) is no worse.
>
> I find I will be unable to live on $400 a year. We lived as economically as we know how but were unable to make both ends meet. We have practically spent nothing on clothes and will have to this year. I have not spent $5 on clothes for Lillie since we married and but about $25 or $30 for myself in that time. Do you think we could stand to raise my allowance?

Business did improve. The letter of January, 1892, the letterhead was "Gray and Smith, dealers in Lumber and Grain, Coal, Paints, Salt Brick, Lime, Cement, etc. Neosho Falls, Woodson County, Kansas." By October of 1893, Matt Smith was able to buy out his financial partner, William Gray, and the letters to stopped. In time, the M. R. Smith Lumber Company succeeded, and the Smith sons grew into positions of responsibility. My grandfather left the company and grew his own lumber company so well that at his death, he was able to endow the foundation that I administer, which is rewarding work. When I read the letters from my great grandfather, I am humbled by his struggles.

The previous fall, I had visited the towns mentioned in Matt's letters and mined what information I could from the libraries and cemetery records. Now it was time to meet Cousin Bill.

Cousin Bill had some more of his grandmother Fanny's letters for me to peruse. Girl talk, he had said in his note inviting me to visit, but I hoped the letters would mention how Matt and his mother arrived in Kansas. There was a big gap in what I knew of their history.

Bill's office occupied a small, two-story brick office building on a side street. The door was ajar when I arrived, so I pushed it in and entered. The ground floor was open with two tiny side rooms and a stairway in the rear. A well-worn patterned rug defined a space in front of an old table, which was surrounded by several heavy, scarred chairs. In the back were shelves loaded with dusty books and unruly piles of papers and magazines. The paintings on the walls were beautiful images of birds: ducks, plovers and snipe. Doors into two side rooms were open, lights on, but no Bill. Finally, I called up the stairs, and a muffled voice answered.

I saw his polished shoes first, descending the creaking stairs. The rest of him was tall, slim and silvery.

"Well. At last we meet. What a pleasure." He greeted me with a big smile and a handshake.

"I was upstairs going through more boxes of letters, but didn't find what I was hunting for. Come on into my office."

In the rear side-room, he cleared a stack of books off a second chair for me, and sat in his well-worn swivel chair.

I had been shy about seeking him out, but surprisingly, we had a fair amount in common. To my birdwatching adventures he replied, "Oh, I like birds, too. Until recently, I used to hunt them."

He spoke calmly, looking at me. I reserved any judgment, and he continued, "Then I had a change of heart as I grew older. They are so beautiful. Back then, I used to tow my 24-foot trailer over to Wyoming for years in the fall, up over those mountain passes. Yes, I would set it up, and my hunting friends would come to join me. I loved that life." He paused. "I had strict rules for the others, though. It was my trailer, so they had to do what I said. Kept it neat that way." He was like my controlling grandfather in that way.

He told me he was writing a memoir and wanted to read what I was writing. I promised that when I returned home I'd send him a short piece I'd had published dealing with my experiences of killing, from bedbugs to sheep.

I packed the little bag of letters into Turtle, promising to return them after I'd mined any tidbits. I'm not finished yet. Handwritten letters are charming but difficult to decipher.

In the evening, I visited Bill at his house to meet his wife and his daughter, a cheerful woman about my age. She and Bill joked easily, but I could see his sadness at her planned move to Arizona.

I was able to fill them in on a few details about Matt Smith they didn't know and they gave me key birth and death dates for my records and fleshed out activities of the current family. After searching in isolation for my ancestors, it was fun to swap stories with someone who was as interested as I was in them.

October 25, Kansas

The night before I left Chanute, I listened to the weather report to decide my route for the next day. Thunderstorms were possible around Wichita. The Texas panhandle had tornadoes. Cousin Bill had suggested I take Highway 54 to avoid traffic.

The only store open really early in the morning was Wal-Mart and I needed another book to read. I don't like to patronize Wal-Mart because I know how often their stores on the edge of small towns drive local retailers out of business. I'd also read that the company regularly took advantage of their employees by requiring them to work off the clock when they completed their eight-hour shifts. But, it is difficult to always act on principles.

I plucked Frank McCourt's *'Tis* from a bookrack of pulp romances. I wonder who filed it in that category. When I looked around for a cashier, the store seemed deserted. Then I heard distant laughter. Applause. More laughs. Then a rising chant, a call and response. I strained to hear the words, but only caught the mix of muddled voices. It was the Wal Mart staff, the corporate rev-up, serve-those-customers-well meeting. The clerk who finally appeared had a smiley face, so I guess the pep rally worked for her, but I wondered how often she had been required to work off the clock.

I took Bill's suggestion and jogged a bit north to pick up Highway 54. In spite of my precautions, I had to pull over east of El Dorado, Kansas to let a fierce downpour pass. My weather radio said there were thunderstorms over Wichita, as well, about 35 miles ahead of me.

Back on the road, I passed several red tailed hawks hunched on the overhead wires and posts that lined the road, the only perches for them in that flat land. Their wings were cocked half open and their feathers were fluffed. Poor things. They looked so miserable, was I anthropomorphizing? Do they know what misery is? Do they feel the joy I would if I could soar, lifting myself without effort on air currents? Doubtful. They are birds. This is their life.

At the Twin Burger in Kingman, three locals nursed their coffees and compared high water stories. Three inches fell in the last twenty-four hours, they said. Fields were flooded and the creeks were rising fast. In town, many basements had water running through them.

My milkshake was so thick, I couldn't even get it through the straw. Made from real ice cream.

At almost 5 p.m. a black cloud boiled high into the sky a little to the right of my path. A gray curtain of heavy rain hung under the cloud, so I pulled into Bloom Rest Stop. A truck and trailer sat to one side, but there was no driver in sight. Sleeping? Maybe cautious like me.

I parked Turtle next to a small rest room solidly built out of cement blocks. Right next to my window, a cedar bush taller than my eye level lashed wildly in the wind. A flock of house sparrows had taken shelter there, hanging on with their tiny feet. They lunged with the flailing branches as if riding bucking horses, fluttering to stay upright. One bird let go, and flapped frantically against the wind to finally regain the same bush. The birds clinging to the branches carefully sidestepped into the interior of their shelter, always keeping a firm grip with one foot.

I watched the heavy cloud in my rear view mirror. It was blacker than when I first saw it and it was moving rapidly in my direction. I turned on my weather radio. A tornado alert had been declared for Ford County until 5pm. Where was Ford County, I wondered? I checked my map. I was *in* Ford County. I listened again as the nasal computer voice announced:

"The National Weather Service Doppler radar in Dodge City indicates the chance of a brief tornado in east Ford County. If a thunder storm is in your vicinity, take shelter now."

I looked around me. That cloud sure qualified. Cars whizzed by on Highway 54. Why weren't they taking shelter?

A few minutes later, my nasal companion said, "This is a dangerous storm. A tornado alert is in effect until 5:30. Move into your underground shelter now."

I locked Turtle and hurried into the sturdy rest room. There was no place to sit except for the toilets in the three stalls, so I crouched against the wall in the disabled stall.

"Don't stay in mobile homes. They offer no protection," said the voice from the radio now lying on the floor.

I recalled news images of flimsy mobile homes ripped apart after tornadoes, but Turtle isn't a mobile home. She's much sturdier. But I still felt safer inside, if there really was danger out in that wind. I turned off the radio to save the batteries and to pass the time, I practiced a few yoga positions. I kept an ear perked for a car motor. A newcomer, finding me standing on one foot, arms outstretched, would probably be too surprised to stay, and under the circumstances, I wouldn't mind a little company.

At 5:31 p.m. I switched on the radio again. A real voice was talking about a blizzard in northwest Kansas, snowdrifts as high as 8 feet, many cattle lost. Egad. What was going on? My heart thumped heavily until the narrator finished and recapped that the blizzard occurred several years ago.

Then, the tinny voice returned and said the tornado alert had expired.

I struggled to open the heavy door to the outside. The wind had calmed somewhat and the black cloud was now to the east. I climbed back into Turtle. Out my window, I could hear the sparrows having loud discussions. They'd pause for reflection and start up again, still on their bucking branches.

Three men casting lines into the lake next to their truck were the only occupants of the campground. That didn't feel like a safe place to stop for the night so I continued on to a rest stop north of Liberal, Kansas. From the bare spots and nighttime activity, it was popular place, and thus I reasoned, safe enough for me to sleep. Activity was the key. If no one knew I was camped in an isolated spot, I felt safe. But if my presence was known and I didn't know the area, I felt too vulnerable to sleep well. Maybe it was the name of the town that suggested safety. Cowboys on the western cattle trails that passed nearby had deemed that area uninhabitable, but the first homesteader, Mr. S.S. Rogers, was generous to passing travelers by providing them with water without charge. "That's mighty liberal of you," they would say. When Mr. Rogers opened a general store with a post office, Liberal seemed a good name for the new town.

Optima National Wildlife Refuge in the panhandle of Oklahoma lay close to my path for the next day. I didn't have a reference for that refuge, but there was a reservoir and a campground marked on my map. The morning began in bright sunlight, but as I approached the refuge, wisps of fog licked the road. When the fog thickened, I turned on my flashers for safety. I drove slowly, hardly able to see past the edge of the pavement until finally the fog thinned, and I was surprised to find myself on the dam that formed Optima Lake.

The campground and hiking trails were laid out below the dam. The weather had improved, so I tied on my hiking shoes and stepped onto a newly scraped path that led up the nearest hill into desert scrub. Sagging dew-pearled webs hung between old thistle stalks, and the musty smell of last summer's wet grass filled the air. A whirring of wings startled me as I rounded the shoulder of a hill. An owl glided up over a notch and out of sight. It had to have been sitting in the only bare and stumpy tree I could see. I missed a good look, and chided myself for my inattentive blundering along the path.

At the top of the next rise, I could hear a slow poc-poc-poc muted by the thinning fog. It sounded like the one-cylinder engine of a friend's funky motorboat, a one-lung diesel he called it. I peered toward the sound and made out a lone oil pump on the top of the next rise, the rocker arm going up and down in rhythm to the popping of the motor. While I caught my breath, I mused on this intrusion. The rig was outside the fence that defined the park. I have an ethereal belief system that I use in wild areas that allows me to believe the wildness goes on forever, uninterrupted by human intervention but, this pump was incongruent with my preferred image of wilderness. Oh, well. I tried for the integration my yoga teacher used when a truck goes by during a meditative moment. "Take in all the sounds and make them a part of your practice," she has said many times. The sound of the pump was gentle, not overpowering, so I allowed it in as a part of the scene. Besides, it reminded my of a favorite toy I had as a child. It was a silly plastic bird with a tuft of yellow feathers for a tail mounted on a pivot so it dipped forward like the rocker arm of the oilrig. The beak of the bird dipped into a little cup of water and stayed there for a moment, and then rocked back up. It demonstrated properties of water tension, but I just liked to watch it bob and dip.

The sun and fog fought for dominance as I descended into the wetland thick with willows and poplars drinking the trickle of water from the dam. A soft breeze rattled the hard, dry leaves. A man and his happy young golden retriever passed me on their way up the hill. We smiled and he hurried to keep up with the romping puppy. The strangled call of sandhill cranes drifted from somewhere beyond the dam.

Refreshed, I drove Turtle up to the dam level to find a small flock of white pelicans circling up from the surface of the water, but no cranes. I saw some shelters on a bluff overlooking the lake and drove around to the picnic area. The fat, gray bodies of the cranes blended well against the islands of mud. I could not see them until one cried out, and leaped into the air with the long legs and neck and the grace of a ballet dancer. When it landed beside its three friends I caught a flash of its crimson forehead, but when I looked away, I lost them again though I could still hear the resonant, wooden rattle of their call.

It didn't take long to complete the forty-mile traverse of the Oklahoma panhandle. Approaching Dalhart, Texas, the announcer on the local station read the pig prices, high school football scores and an ad for Mama's candle shop. This was oil country, filled with pick-ups and cowboy hats, jeans and boots. Flat-roofed motels and "eateries" lined the intersecting roads. At the Dairy Queen, I sucked on my milkshake and watched the people come and go. A young woman in tight jeans trailed two pre-school boys barely able to swagger in their cowboy boots, and wearing big cowboy hats held up by their doubled-over ears.

Another pair of customers came around the corner from behind the building. The gray-whiskered man propped his ancient, fat tired bike against the back wall of the DQ. He touched the head of his shaggy companion with affection. She followed him to the entrance. He looked once more at her and went inside, leaving her to gaze at him through the door. She watched him for a moment and then turned to sniff the detritus in the parking lot. Finding nothing edible, she returned to check the bike, sniffed it, went back to the door to flop down and stare through the glass again, her mongrel yellow ears pricked, alert for his return.

Outside of Moriarty, New Mexico on I-40, a red neon "RV Camp" caught my attention. It was so unassuming in its simplicity I knew I would like the place. Zia RV Campground was a little run down, but that's better than flash. Multiple layers of paint held the office porch together where a pleasant youngish man took my money and went over the amenities they had to offer. I missed most of what he said, tired after a long day.

The graveled site was close enough to level and after getting set up, I headed for the shower. I passed a pen of pygmy goats, some playing and some begging from the top of a hillock of dirt. The owners recycle, and a sign next to the goats asked for table scraps and the goats watched me closely until it was clear I had nothing to offer them. Free-range chickens scratched the dirt unbothered by the many cats that wandered the grounds. "Eggs for sale in the office," another sign said.

The floor in the shower/laundry wing was springy, but the shower was hot and free. After a lovely clean up, I searched for the guy who took my money when I signed in to buy some laundry soap. I could see him and his sweetie next to the fence at the edge of the park, gazing at the rolling hills beyond. The pig and chickens in the nearby pens were munching their dinner and the couple stood, shoulders touching, enjoying the view out into the desert. The sun cast enchanting shadows across the expanse. They chatted. He threw a few rocks. She put her arm around his waist and they laughed. They reminded me of my back-to-the-land days when I was married. There is something peaceful about raising animals, a daily rhythm you can count on with enough variation so you don't get bored.

When I purchased my soap, I was focused on my laundry, but afterward, I wondered what their story was. Most RV park hosts are older couples who have had to hang up their keys and stay put, or retired folks who roam in the off months. He had a pronounced limp, so maybe they bought it with his disability insurance. Or maybe they inherited the park from an eccentric relative.

After I loaded the washer, I poked around the multipurpose room. A stack of photocopied brochures next to the washing machine promoted the amenities of this modest RV park, which included a book exchange: two short lines of rumpled paperbacks in a wobbly bookshelf, and Tammy's fitness course: steps and obstacles along the fence that add up to one mile by repeating segments.

After dark, a big rig showed up; pulled into the spot to my right. Forty feet long, at least. I ate my dinner and watched the set up. First, a little whirring as the leveling legs descend. Then the graying couple emerged, carefully climbing down, protecting arthritic joints. Set up that TV dish first. That's her job. He hooks up the power, water and sewer. She pulls out the step and lays the mat on the ground below it to scrape off the dirt. Some catchy phrase, "Welcome to Our Home," "Corgis Welcome Here," or "Cat Lover." No talking needed.

Then, another rig equally as large pulled in to the space to my left. I was book ended. I grabbed *The Guide to National Wildlife Refuges* and retired to my cozy nest to read up on Bosque del Apache Wildlife Refuge, 80 miles south of Albuquerque, a Mecca for birders and my goal for the next day.

October 27, New Mexico

Thousands of birds winter over at Bosque del Apache NWR or pass through on their migrations. *Bosque* means woods or forest, and the Indians stopped there to hunt when the birds were plentiful. The refuge is located at the northern edge of the Chihuahuan desert, and straddles the Rio Grande River. The heart of the refuge is an active flood plain, and the refuge managers are restoring the extensive wetlands, farmlands and riparian zones.

In the bookstore, a friendly volunteer helped me enlarge my birding library with two recently published books, *Birds of North America* by Ken Kaufman with computer-manipulated pictures meant for beginners, and *The Sibley Guide to Birds* by David Allen Sibley, for which the author gathered more avian information than previously available in one book. The listings are accompanied by Sibley's beautifully detailed illustrations. Though it was written for the experienced aficionado, I hoped I could grow into it.

After my visits to many wildlife refuges, I learned here how much care went into managing them. Each of the many ponds was at a different stage of development, which replicates the evolution of a natural pond, beginning with open water that gradually fills in with lake vegetation until it becomes a meadow. Then, the refuge managers dig it out to begin again. Throughout, the refuge ponds are available for the various birds: deep water for divers like buffleheads, cormorants and grebes, shallower water for dunkers like most ducks, islands for night safety for cranes, and reeds where soras and rails can hide.

Smartweed, millet, chufa, bullrush and sedges are planted for bird food. In nearby fields, local farmers are paid to plant alfalfa and corn, harvesting the alfalfa and leaving the corn for wildlife. By pushing ripe stalks of corn to the ground to make the grain more accessible to the birds, the numbers of birds in any area can be controlled to reduce the risk of diseases from overcrowding. Willow and cottonwood bosques that line the Rio Grand River have been invaded by non-native tamarisk and salt cedar. Refuge staff is clearing those and replanting with cottonwood, black willow and other native species to restore the native bosques.

I took a copy of the map showing the hiking trails and network of roads that rim the ponds back to Turtle. Driving the roads, I noticed volunteers clumped in groups of three or four who were doing their monthly species population count. I joined a group of three silver hairs who were peering over a pond that looked devoid of life. Their terse comments made it clear they were far more experienced than I was. One woman told me they were looking for diving birds that are hard to count because they only surface briefly between dives. She interrupted herself to point out a horned grebe that had come up for air. It looked around for only a moment before doing a lovely kip and dive back down into the water. I waited with them for half an hour, but they had more patience than I did, so I moved on. I guess I still had the patience lesson to learn.

In the afternoon, I hiked down an abandoned dirt road into the scrub on the east side of the refuge. I got exercise, all right. October had been a wet month and it was still hot and humid. The mosquitoes found me. I had taken my binoculars, hoping for some songbirds in the brush, but in only a few minutes, I knew this was a survival hike. NO stopping. I had to walk as fast as I could so the mini-wind I generated would keep them from landing. I returned to Turtle sticky and frustrated.

I drove into Socorro, the nearest town, while the birds had their siesta, and when I returned I tried the other hiking trail. This time I draped a bright yellow kanga over my head and shoulders. The light cotton cloth provided better air circulation around my arms than long sleeves and it covered my ears as well as my head. I was still a little warm but all that flowing material confused the hell out of the little buggers. The bright African print probably would have scared anyone I met as well, but the few people on the refuge stayed in their cars.

As the heat let up, flocks of sandhill cranes flew from one field to the next, and then back, chortling and gurgling. Some birds plopped on the grass, gray mounds of feathers, heads still high. I had just learned that they sleep on islands for protection from coyotes, so maybe they were just napping.

My last stop was near an observation blind, a wooden wall set under a shady tree next to a pond. When I quietly lifted a panel to peek into the water on the other side, the water birds were so close I hardly needed my binoculars: mallard-sized redheads, canvasbacks, gadwalls and the smaller western and pied billed grebes. Sitting together on a log, double-crested and neotropic cormorants. Magic.

Double crested cormorants are common on the Oregon coast, and I know them by their orange face and rather punk-like flash of feathers over the eye during breeding season. Another viewer who seemed to know the cormorant varieties pointed out the smaller size and longer tail of the neotropic cormorant, and its paler face. Rarely, is it possible to compare two such similar birds. That moment was a gift.

At the RV park, a flock of Gambel's quail entertained me. Who cannot love those pudgy little birds that poke about, pecking here and there, muttering to each other and jiggling the teardrop plumes on their heads? They were so tame I could study their markings against the picture in my books. They are very similar to California quail, but are a paler gray with a buff colored breast.

The next day, I made a quick loop around the ponds, and the refuge was deserted of both birds and people. I would have been disappointed if I had only come that day and realized again that birdwatching is only a point in time. Some days you see them, and some days you don't. The morning was cool and bugless, so I drove to the edge of the refuge for a vigorous desert walk before the day's drive.

Almost 300 miles got me to Willcox in southeastern Arizona for the night. The next day, I birded in the Chiracaua National Monument, a rich biological area at the intersection of the Chihuahuan and Sonoran deserts, and the southern Rocky Mountains and northern Sierra Madre in Mexico.

Up the side of a wooded valley, at a hairpin curve in the trail, a bridled titmouse hung on the end of a fir branch. Another easy identification with its soft gray body, the crest and the black and white bridle pattern on its face. A saucy Mexican jay and shy red-naped sapsucker lurked along the trail to a campground, and the startled white eyes of an acorn woodpecker followed me as I strolled along the creek. All firsts for me.

At the campground, I noticed the metal bear-proof boxes and I wondered if Turtle could look like a food box to a bear. Not a pretty thought.

I stayed two days in Tucson to visit my uncle and his wife. My Uncle Ralph is graying and favors a bum hip when he walks, but he still has the droll laugh I knew when we both were much younger, the same laugh I heard when he showed the old film of the moose hunt with his father. He and his wife, Jay, were delighted to show me around their desert-landscaped yard and I kept my eye out for birds, of course. A California quail sat atop a nearby post and repeatedly claimed his territory. Through my binoculars, I watched a huge mouth open for the vocalization, but the sound that emerged was a muted, even dainty, "wow."

Jay pointed out a Saguaro Cactus on a neighbor's land where she had seen a pair of birds nesting in the spring. She got out their binoculars and we waited. Soon, a bird flew to the tall cactus and perched on top, scanning the desert floor for movement. It was an American kestral, a small falcon, with its characteristic vertical eye stripe. They often sit on wires, but in that area, all the utilities are underground and the cacti were the tallest points around.

Ralph is the same generation as Cousin Bill in Chanute. With my conversations with Bill in mind, I compared Bill's perception of my grandfather with my uncle's. The Chanute branch of the family knew of my grandfather primarily through his success as a businessman, and a man generous with his extended family. When he was able, my grandfather gave shares of company stock to family and employees. When the company had cash, he would declare a dividend on those shares. He often hired relatives, but they had to prove themselves capable or they did not last. One of the Gray boys had not made the cut, and the family remembers, but seemed to hold no grudge.

My grandfather had hoped Uncle Ralph would take over the business, according to my father who worked for him. When I was in high school, I knew my grandfather was close to selling to Diamond Match. Then one day, my father came home and announced the deal was off. Young Ralph had apparently showed some sign enough for my grandfather to think he might have a spark of interest in the company. But it didn't last, and the company was sold later to Kimberly-Clark. My Uncle Ralph chose to pursue a Ph.D. in physics, about as far from a business career as I can imagine.

My mother is ten years older than her brother. She spent a great deal of time with their father at a time when he was starting his company. When she turned sixteen, she was recruited to help drive on his many trips to the west coast from Kansas City. The roads were unpaved and the cars were not air-conditioned, and he would stop often to talk with the men at lumberyards who were buying his products. By the time my uncle became a teenager, his father traveled more often by train, and did not need a driver, perhaps to their mutual loss.

When these elders die, these stories will be forgotten. Their names will be entered into the family tree with their birth, marriage and death data and become links between the past and present, the richness of their lives lost to those who follow.

The next day, I birded Agua Calient Park, where I saw my first vermillion flycatcher, a speck of vibrant color, visible without binoculars from an astonishing distance. At the Saguaro Desert Museum I sat in the birdcage and studied the captives. The pyrrhuloxia is a cardinal with much more gray on its body than a northern cardinal, and the bill is stubbier and yellow rather than red-orange. The saucy phainopepla, though not in the cardinal family, looks like a slim, glossy-black cardinal with a sharper black bill and ragged crest. I also saw a crissal thrasher in the cage, which might have been the bird that stumped me at Agua Caliente, though I couldn't retain the markings in my head for a good comparison. At least, I saw the long curved bill. Counting the caged birds as sightings was against my principles, but I could study them at close range for future reference.

In the hummingbird cage the sparkling jewels zipped from branch to branch. When they perched, the tiny birds were well hidden. Unless I saw them land or they moved, I could be staring right at them and not see anything in the patterns of leaves. At the red feeders, their wings blurred and their thread-like tongues eagerly licked the sweet water. Outside, a wild hummer attacked me by flying aggressively into my face, wanting me to move away from another feeder I'd almost hit with my head. I stood motionless as it drank, three feet from me.

October 31, Arizona

I said goodbye to Ralph and Jay and started north on my final leg home. I hadn't stopped birding, however. At a rest stop, a plaintive three-note whistle drew me into the thorny shrubs where I found a verdin, as tiny as a bushtit, with dull gray plumage and yellow head and throat.

The rest of the day was a long drive.

The next day, east of Lake Havasu in the Bill Williams River National Wildlife Refuge, I drove down one of the access roads beside a dry creek bed. Tamarisk and cottonwoods reached into the earth to suck for the subterranean water. I stopped to check for birds, spotted one on the top of a tree, and the name "Loggerhead Shrike" popped into my head. I looked it up in my book, and that's what it was. I could be a birder yet. Loggerhead shrikes are the size of a robin with a stubby, hooked bill, gray back and head with a black mask over its eyes and black on its wings. It has the unusual habit of impaling small creatures that it catches on barbed wire or cactus spines because its feet lack strength and agility of a raptor's. So in their habitat, it is not unusual to see half a lizard or mouse spiked on a fence, a shrike's doggy bag.

A sign further on warned not to continue without four-wheel drive, so I parked and walked on. Turtle could have handled most of the road, all except for the ten-foot dip that would have hung her on her bumpers. That's all it takes.

I would have loved to spend the night in that quiet and deserted spot. It felt safe. But it's illegal to camp on a wildlife refuge, and I'm a good girl. I stopped on my way out for a covey of Gamble's Quail that moseyed down the road in front of me. Individuals paused now and again for a refreshing dust bath at the edge of the road, unconcerned about the vehicle that waited patiently for them. They talked among themselves, in no hurry, and I smiled.

In the Sacramento Valley, I slowed to enjoy glorious fall weather and the wildlife on several refuges. Thousands of birds filled the ponds: snowy egrets, white pelicans, ruddy ducks, snow geese, greater white fronted geese as well as the more common birds, Canada geese, mallards, pintails, green-wing and blue-wing teals. Pheasants paraded across the refuge roads and cried from the dense grass. The abundance was breathtaking.

In Tucson, I had called my house sitter to alert her of my impending arrival, but I was moving faster than I had anticipated, so I turned west at Redding, to cross the Coast Range. My first hermit thrush sat at the bottom of a little bush by a stream near the crest of the mountains, unperturbed, while I fumbled in my bird books. On the coast, I tried to identify some scoters bobbing in the surf. Looking down from a bluff, I watched their rolling motion through my binoculars and felt queasy. All I could see was their black bodies and large heavy bills, but not the key markings, which would tell me which kind of scoter they were. I resolved to buy a spotting scope when I got home.

The days were glorious and I affirmed the thrill of birding, both for finding the birds and for where I found myself: coastal bluffs, dikes, open fields, shaded forest paths, and ponds full of noise and feathers.

Turtle climbed the rugged Oregon headlands and skirted the long white beaches. Though I've driven the Oregon coast many times, the scenery on a sunny day always leaves me breathless. I took several short beach hikes, enjoying the light wind and sea air. I remembered how difficult it was to get to the shore in Newport and Bar Harbor and loved being back in my home state, where the beach is literally accessible to everyone, though only a few people take advantage of it at any one time.

Don's Ice Cream & Cafe in Florence was a good choice for lunch. Plastic buckets for $1.50. Weather beautiful. It was hard to believe it was November.

November 5, 2000 Home Again

When I drove into my driveway, I was thrilled to be home again and also disappointed that the trip was over. Nothing dramatic, just over. My cat welcomed me as if I'd been out shopping so I knew my house sitter had done her job well. The garden was a bit weedy and the lawn needed mowing, but most everything else was as I had left it two months previously.

When I pulled my box of souvenirs from under the passenger seat I fingered the blocky sandstone rock from Lake Champlain, the hickory nut from Primehook National Wildlife Refuge in Delaware, the sea-tossed oyster shell from Pea Island, North Carolina, fossilized Illinois limestone, the beaver gnawed wood chip, a fluff of raw southeastern cotton, a Wisconsin pinecone, the multi-colored Vermont maple leaves, and a piece of pine bark from Natural Bridge, Alabama. At the touch of every physical remembrance from my trip, scenes of the locations where I found them burst into my head.

The variety and richness of my journey left me feeling full and satisfied. So many of the things that had worried me before leaving had either not happened, or I had coped quite well and they faded away. I had driven almost 14,000 miles in two months and had a glorious time.

Already, I was thinking about my next trip. More time in the places I whizzed through for certain. Mexico? Canada? Alaska? Places with open space and few people appealed to me. Or should I improve my conversation skills, and actually talk to people, try to figure out those pesky dangling questions *before* I left a spot.

The end is only the beginning.

Post Script

The following summer on July 3, found me east of Alturas, California. The valley floor was hot and humid, parched after a dry spring. By midafternoon, birding was fruitless as the birds waited quietly for the relief of evening shadows. I pointed Turtle in the direction of the nearby Warner Mountains to find refuge from the scorched fields of grass and baked-mud lakes.

Turtle's motor labored as we climbed into the dry pine forests. All the isolated backwoods camping spots were already occupied by holiday campers, and at Soap Spring Campground, only a few spaces were left among the large motor homes and trailers. Barbeques, satellite dishes, ATV's, dogs, kids and piles of stuff cluttered the sites. Campers were dug in for serious fun in the woods. I had left the urban chaos of the San Francisco Bay area the previous day, and here it was again.

Back on the graveled forest road we climbed across the side of a hill. It was getting late, and I was beginning to worry that we might not find a spot for the night when I noticed a dirt track in the valley below me. It emerged from behind the shoulder of a distant hill, rimmed a meadow and came up to join the road I was on not far ahead of me. I nosed Turtle to the edge of this new road, got out and peered down. Fresh tire marks indicated recent use. No sign told me where the summer road led, but it was worth exploring. I urged Turtle forward, and for a moment, all I could see was air in front of me. Savoring the rush from plunging into open space, I crept down into the valley. I kept an eye out for places to turn around, in case the track became impassable. Near the little hill that had swallowed the track, I found a spot wide enough for someone to pass where a stand of pines shielded me from the road above. The danger of fire lurked everywhere that summer and I was careful to park Turtle so no dry grass touched her hot underbelly.

I turned off the motor, waited and listened. Would someone appear and tell me to move? Was there some reason why this divine spot was still available? The mosquitoes were neither abundant nor aggressive, so I threw open Turtle's doors to let her cool off after her long climb. The air temperature was still over 80 degrees, humidity about the same. After some tidying and a snack, I felt secure enough to risk a shower. I hung the plastic bag of water from Turtle's back door, stripped and rinsed off the day's sweat-salt and dust. The cool water slid over my sticky skin.

I felt marvelously clean and refreshed.

I considered reading, studying maps or writing in my journal, but decided to just sit and absorb my surroundings. The side step of my van is my front porch and I settled in. Clumps of pines to the left and far to the right framed the view. Gray-green sagebrush and tawny grass filled the mountain meadow, which was about 7000 feet above sea level, making the final rise of the high desert mountains in the distance seem like hills. They were covered with more sagebrush and a few scattered pines. A brutally broken, twisted trunk of a young tree was the only indication that the meadow had been covered deep in snow only a few months before.

To the south, a lightning bolt flickered under roiling cumulus clouds, which hinted of rain. The delayed sound of thunder was only a soft grumble. If the rain reached me, I might have had to move Turtle back onto the graveled road or risk getting mired in mud, but I doubted it would. It looked like the kind of dry storm that starts forest fires, but sends no rain to quench the flames.

The plaintive song of a mountain chickadee, one long note followed by two lower and shorter ones, drifted from the pines. At the descending *peeeeuw* of a red tailed hawk, I turned to see the big raptor flap to the top of a pine and grab a frail branch that sagged with the weight. He swayed there only briefly before sailing off over the crest of the hill to continue his hunt.

The sun sank behind the mountains and the sting of the direct rays faded. An erratic light breeze played through the new sagebrush growth, releasing a pungent fragrance into the evening. Occasional puffs of cool air tickled my skin. Sleep would soon be possible.

Feathery cirrus clouds high above me caught the light from the hidden sun and turned a pale pink.

I imagined I was the first person to find that meadow. I wondered if the actual first visitor had followed the deer trails, like the one I could see from my perch. Did he find water for his night's pause? Did he have meat for supper? How did he start his fire? Or was it a woman who first challenged this wilderness? Perhaps seeking roots and bulbs for her family?

A family of mule deer browsed in my direction from behind the pines to my left. With a start, the buck snatched his head up and locked his brown eyes on Turtle. Ears flicked, and then pointed forward, alert. Soft nostrils flared. He huffed and sniffed for clues.

Then, he waggled his stumpy tail and lowered his head, displaying his small rack of velvety antlers. I watched, hardly breathing. Cautiously, he stepped his tiny hoof into the road. A doe and a half-grown fawn followed, watching both him and Turtle, more curious than cautious. I loved this intimate contact, yet I wanted to scare them away so they would fear vehicles. Fall would arrive all too soon, and trucks would bring guns. When the fawn, last in line, had crossed the road, as if on a signal, they threw their heads high and pronged away over the sagebrush.

The sky intensified to salmon so slowly the change was hard to notice, and then it softened to a deep rose. Color faded to shades of gray, and finally, all I could see was the dark silhouette of the hilltops against the stars emerging from the darkening sky.

I felt porous, without barriers. The essence of the place flowed through me. I belonged there.

In Appreciation

My sincerest thanks go to those who helped me along the way to this first book. Judith Barrington got my attention by saying that every woman had a story to tell, and was patient with my first writing attempts. Many fellow writers in workshops and writing groups gave me invaluable encouragement and astute critiques that built skills and confidence. Sandra Dorr, my editor, gave me wonderful ideas for fleshing out a travel journal into a thoughtful and researched narrative.

Thanks go to my brother for his all-important detailed reading of the text and his computer expertise for the preparation of the photos and illustrations. He also gets credit for the author photo. Special appreciation goes to my mother, who loves anything I write, a quality every writer needs at certain points in the process.